Copyright © 2018 Tekkan
Artwork Copyright © 2018

All rights reserved.
First Printing, 2018
ISBN 978-0-998-18993-2

To contact Tekkan please email:
buddhaboy1289@gmail.com

Table of Contents

Everyday Mind I . . . . Page 1

Everyday Mind II. . . . . Page 105

Everyday Mind III. . . . . Page 206

Asphalt Driveway Co.. . . . . Page 206

Shakespeare and Zen . . . . Page 218

Scootering in Kyoto . . . . Page 226

Continents . . . . Page 241

Philadelphia . . . . Page 255

Cottonwood Poems . . . . Page 260

Politics . . . . Page 270

Myths and Dreams . . . . Page 288

Indra's Net . . . . Page 299

Heart Sutra . . . . Page 303

Everyday Mind IV. . . . . Page 308

Utopia . . . . Page 404

Everyday Mind V . . . . Page 411

Dragonfly . . . . Page 413

Lascaux Caves . . . . Page 418

Tour de France . . . . Page 425

Circles of Sober Alcoholics. . . . . Page 484

Introduction

Do you know how life sometimes imposes itself on you in a way that's permanent and creates something that changes your orientation, though at the time it's barely noticeable?

It's what happened to me when I was twenty-two-years-old on a trip to Amsterdam, during the Christmas break from my studies in Oxford, England. I took the ferry at Dover, and I rode the trains. I had heard about the red light district in Amsterdam, where women present themselves in windows, and I was on a mission to lose my virginity, which I did.

The summer before my trip was a culmination. I had finished my third summer working on the crews who put in asphalt driveways. I was paying my way through college. It was hard, dangerous labor that we did from the earliest light to evening twilight. The asphalt was steaming hot, and summer afternoons were searing. The men I worked with were rough characters who swore constantly, and I became just like them.

My final year of college I went to St. Michael's Hall, to the Center for Medieval and Renaissance Studies, located on Shoe Lane, around the corner from Christ Church in Oxford. St. Michael's Hall was a school for Americans, and when I arrived, there were snooty students from high-dollar universities all over America.

I immensely enjoyed the expert instruction I experienced in my one-on-one tutorials. I was also overwhelmed by the tremendous lift of my cultural surroundings.

In previous years I had read almost all of Shakespeare's plays, and I especially loved *Hamlet*, *Macbeth*, *King Lear*, and the *Tempest*. However, it was on my way to Amsterdam, while on the trains, the ferry, and waiting for trains in Amsterdam, that I read Shakespeare's sonnets, for the first time.

I can't say what hooked me exactly. Maybe it was the passion Shakespeare conveyed. Or it might have been the ornate, metaphorical language he used. Then again, it might have been his strong and dexterous rhythms.

I admired the storytelling in each sonnet, leading to a surprise ending in the couplet. I loved the puzzling wordiness — it made me scrutinize each word. He was communicating his personal experience, not that of a created character. The world he described was so different from mine that, as I read, I became a time-traveler. It seemed to me that every sonnet was a moving memorial. Being young and inexperienced, the sonnets impacted me.

I was impacted, again, four years later. By that time I had become a drug addict and an alcoholic. After sobering up, and in my second year of recovery, I read a book — *Jobs in Japan*. The book was about going to Japan and teaching English in one of their many language schools. I read *Jobs in Japan* while riding buses up and down University Avenue in St. Paul, Minnesota. Soon after, I got on an airplane and landed in Osaka, a complete stranger to Japanese culture.

What is a lonely guy to do when he goes where everyone looks strange and speaks a foreign language?

It took me six months to find a steady position. I read translations of Japanese poetry while riding trains between Osaka and Kyoto, and while waiting for job interviews in coffee shops. There, I discovered the tanka form. A tanka is a five-line poem invented by the courtly class in the seventh century. Noble men and women wrote each other love poems in the form of a single unbroken sentence. Here is one of Princess Nukata's from the *Manyoshu*:

"While, waiting for you,
My heart is filled with longing,
The autumn wind blows —
As if it were you —
Swaying the bamboo blinds of my door."

The Japanese aren't always direct, but they are concise. Where Shakespeare is wordy, the Japanese are precise and refined — every word contributes to resounding impact.

How to Read My Poems

I have married the sonnet to the tanka. I tell a story in the sonnet — using three quatrains, separated by line spaces, and a final couplet. The story builds to a conclusion in the couplet. The tanka is a commentary, or a counterpoint, to the sonnet — the combined poems have two endings.

I don't rhyme my sonnets, because I want freer expression. I want to be direct in my meaning — I want people to clearly understand my meaning. The metaphors are inspired by Shakespeare, and the (aimed-for) precision is in imitation of Japanese style. Using the sonnet with the tanka, I am mixing the sensibility of the Occident and the Orient — which I have done by living in England, Japan, and America.

I don't punctuate much in my poetry. I want the words themselves to do the work. There is logic between words, and the forms provide structure. By not using punctuation I hope to direct readers to carefully attend to each word — to appreciate the graininess of words.

Reading my poems silently, say, on a bus, a train, or an airplane, and reading them aloud, may be different experiences. The way I've written there's not always a pause intended at the end of the line. Hint: *My poems are to be recited not as lines, but as phrases, and a phrase often overflows the break at the end of a line. I pause and take a breath where it seems natural for me to pause. Another person may pause differently than I do.*

Each single poem is a piece of a mosaic, and it is my hope that the collection of poems form an accurate portrait of consciousness.

Thank You

There are people I would like to thank. Jocelyn my daughter has become a wonderful artist. Her paintings grace this book.

Cid Corman was my mentor in Japan. He led a poetry workshop in my home for several years. I didn't write very much while meeting with Cid, because I didn't have much to say — I hadn't digested my life enough at that point. However, Cid was a good teacher and planted many seeds.

I would like to thank my fellow scribblers who meet once a week to read and hear each others' writings — they have provided me with invaluable edits: Bev Bonn Jonnes, Charly Mullan, David Fabio, Greg Kagan, Judy Appel, Melanie Van Wyhe, Michelle Huber, and Paul Suszko. Every writer needs such a group.

And I would also like to thank Laura Paulisich who helped me produce the book, and who is hosting me on her website: www.laurapaulisich.com.

My friend and partner in poetry, who taught English with me in Japan — Gregory Dunne, said, "In thirty years, if you are still writing sonnets, I'm sure they will be good." I hope he is right.

I am Barry MacDonald. I received the *dharma* name, *Tekkan*, when I took Buddhist vows, which means, Iron Man, a settled practitioner of great determination.

— *Tekkan*

Everyday Mind I

To woo
women

is to
play

and sus-
pend

the
moment;

one

doesn't

hold

control.

June is a memory in November
As I remember the roses and the
Lilacs blooming and the persistence of
The rain the fresh air and the insistence

Of the sun coaxing the season of growth
Along and all the leaves are pristine the
Birds are melodious with the dawn and
The roots of the grass are absorbing the

Rain but now a bitter wind surges through
The trees that stand starkly bare a frosting
Has hardened the ground and the night has grown
Wings and is overshadowing daylight

But none of it matters to me because
Your ebullience overcomes the darkness.

The overcast sky
in November is glowing
because the sun is
always dispensing light and
every day you're radiant.

Stillwater

Iced-over river and overcast sky
Slopes of bare trees and snow the clean cold air
The quiet settled among the bluffs
Prepare this place for reverberations

When the native peoples walked for water
The valley they called "Stillwater" was here
Resonating with creeks and waterfalls
As water spread between limestone bluffs

Sioux and Ojibwa fought in a hollow
Lumberjacks floated rafts of logs downstream
A frontier prison held the Younger Gang
And steamboats plied the townsfolk with supplies —

Pioneer Park has a southward view
For sunrises and sun speckled water.

Sun river
eagle soaring
seeing.

Volition

Mrs. Peterson encouraged me in
High school to read and in the library
I found *Siddhartha* a novel about
An Indian prince contemporary

With the Buddha who began questing for
Awakening by leaving home entering
The woods and meditating and the tale
Inexplicably resonated with

Me and a seed was planted that sprouted
Twenty years later while I taught English
In Japan and met Jim Morton who led
Me to *Hosshinji* a monastery

Where I began seeking enlightenment
Wholeheartedly some thirty years ago.

A leaf opens
to the sun
and I opened
to words
of inspiration.

I like the simplicity of coming
To my *zafu* and *zabuton* on the
Floor sitting with my legs crossed with a straight
Back with my shoulders relaxed and I like

Following my breath and balancing my
Attention allowing thoughts to arise
And letting them go without becoming
Emotional if possible because

I'm sitting as impassively as I
Can but if I become agitated
I practice letting go with the practice
Of motionless posture as if I were

A mountain weathering a thunderstorm
And practice breathing and practice breathing.

Sitting
agitated until
agitation goes
is simple but
not easy.

My mind is a bowl pondering why my
Friend would say he has no one he relies
On because he's never said such hurtful
Words before and my mind is a bowl of

Frustration as I'm plotting to persuade
A woman to submit to my way of
Managing our meager finances as
I consider her quirky reactions

And my mind is a bowl seeing the sun
In a brilliant sky amidst moving clouds
And there suspended is a crescent moon
And for moment I'm just watching as

My mind is a bowl and an opening
Offering good intentions this morning.

Crescent moon
is a hole
in the day
of a blue sky.

As if you and I were assembling
A puzzle together finding pieces
Of our lives scattered on a table and
While drinking coffee we were perusing

Segments of experience and with joy
We discovered commonality and
Compatibility quite surpassing
Ordinary friendliness and so I

Relied on our partnership over time
As we kept connecting the puzzle but
One day you became unapproachable
For no discernable reason I could

Fathom as our friendship dissolved on a
Saturday and you became the puzzle.

Searching for
wholeness
companionship
I want direction
home.

A yellow light spreads on the horizon
As a transparent layering of clouds
Disintegrates in the blue of the sky
Producing tiny crystals of snow as

The sun is rising and snow is shining
The whole sky is changing and who would care
To notice this daily transformation as
Usually I'm busy in traffic or

Immersed in the political news but
See how the sun is a brilliant yellow
The sky has opened and an airliner has
Streaked across leaving contrails drifting and

Seeing the magic in a moment I've
Forgotten ordinary compulsions.

Survival requires
vigorous mastery of
focused energy
yet I want to cultivate
a disengaging talent.

The morning sun shone on the snow on the
Ground and for a moment hundreds of the
Crystals sparkled and the snow became a
Blanket of jewels — in the afternoon as

I drove through town I saw an apple tree
At a modest home decorated with
Dozens of Christmas bulbs in bare branches
Projecting a holiday vibe for me

And even though I was enduring a
Season of scant sun and frigidity
When any exposed skin burned with the cold
As I waited for the heater in my

Car to heat I generated a glow
Of quiet satisfaction and patience.

It takes discipline
to move about in winter
but even amidst the
most austere landscape there are
visions of joyous beauty.

My mind is a bowl of below zero
Cold as I'm following boot prints in the
Shining snow under a blue sky as I'm
Enveloped in a coat with only my

Face burning a little — my mind is a
Bowl and my spine is a staff and my crossed
Legs are foundational for arising
Energy as time and thought are slowed in

Zen — my mind is a bowl and an apple
Tree with half a dozen chickadees just
For a moment as they flutter and go
As I watch from my window and I can

Think of nothing worthier then the birds
As an offering for you this morning.

With nothing between
me and the world I can see
chickadees in the
apple tree and I needn't
think about significance.

The swallow bursts before me snatching my
Sight swooping rising diving and turning
Turning as if it were a whirling blade
Turning and then vanishing into sky —

But the bumblebee lumbers in the grass
Plodding and bumbling and purposeful
Desirous of nectar to return home
Serving the manufacture of the hive —

I can't resist the urge to grab the toad
Squeezing and turning it as I wonder
Is it toads or frogs that give out warts and
I suppose it's either but I don't care —

I've spent an hour playing in summer
And so escaped a dreary winter day.

These blasted days
have frozen my toes
my constantly frozen
toes until this morning's
thaw.

Eric

I remember my first friend beyond my
Family the first intimacy when
We discovered there were secrets to share
And with innocence I gave my trust and

I encountered how much fun it was to
Delve and roam the neighborhood and then my
Family moved to Minnesota and
I left my friend in Kansas — and there was

A procession of friendships and there were
Disappointments and betrayals and I
Had to grow a layer of armor and
I began to measure how much trust was

Sensible and I've tasted bitterness —
But I want to be gentle and sincere.

Wholehearted
innocence was
lost — but I have
circumspection
and kindness.

It's a modest dining room a smallish
Round table and in the morning I make
Coffee and have a bowl of cereal —
Maybe a conversation an email

Or an expression on someone's face from
The day before has left an impression
With me and so I consider what they
Are thinking and how they are coping and

What I should do — I didn't understand
How to direct my energy when young
How to discover what needs attention —
I come to my breakfast table as to

A reliable sanctuary and
Continuously find intuition.

Solitude is good
regularity helpful
quiet conducive
for the cultivation of
insightful understanding.

The Accident

As winter is dragging on and darkness
Is dominating morning and evening
I became frustrated being stuck in
The little rooms within my little house

So I was blasé this morning in the
Bathroom when I opened the cabinet
And the trimmer fell out into the sink
And I didn't care and I didn't think

Until I trimmed off half my beard and I
Realized the fall had changed the settings
And then what could I do but shave the rest
Even though I was watching the daily

Progression of my winter beard and now
I have to begin all over again.

Or maybe not but
I will certainly
go to a barber
to get a haircut
and restore balance.

To live in proximity with you for
Thirty years has determined so much of
What's emerged as I'm driving you to work
Because your car's being repaired with my

Habitual quiet with you chatting
About who's gossiping about whom and
Who's attending to their cell phones and not
Working about the squirrel you've named "Chub

Chub" that some of you are feeding by the
Dumpster about what you set your heart on
About how you formulate words about
My mind wandering and you asking a

Question and it's hard to imagine
The ride going another direction.

So we discuss what's
going to happen later in
the day when you need
picking up and when we need
to do the weekly shopping.

Balancing so I hear you and not the
Television balancing so I hear
The meaning of your words before forming
A response balancing how I wanted

To use this time with your apparent need
To communicate now balancing so
I see my thinking and emotion so
My behavior is appropriate so

I'll have no cause for regret and so I
May see how I might do something worthy
To alleviate conflicting schedules
Or perhaps to just listen to you share

Your experience of this day because
It's so important to live together.

An everyday poise
opening awareness
seeing within me
and seeing circumstances
is a transforming practice.

So it swells into a drop of water
Precariously under the faucet
Separating and falling and bursting
With a plunk in the hollow of the sink

And I can't think of anything to do
To prevent the next drop from forming and
Plunking in the sink except to call a
Plumber as the monotonous plopping

Punctuates the spacious kitchen with a
Plink pointing to a problem needing a
Solution I don't have as I'm not so
Mechanically inclined but suddenly

I remember to get the pliers and
Unscrew the ending and clean the filter.

I've reestablished
quiet and serenity
in the household but
I don't smile triumphantly
As who knows what's coming next?

I couldn't get you to be quiet and
Couldn't persuade you not to lash out at
Him couldn't even intervene to keep
The two of you from arguing as I

Was witnessing the obvious damage
Occurring as both of you were building
Resentments deepening a pattern that
Has disrupted your lives so I will look

For an opening when I can say please
Try to forget about who's right and wrong
Try to regain some composure because
It's much more important at the moment —

But I know from experience there's not
Much I can do to keep you from fighting.

When I'm the target
of someone's anger I want
to fight back even
though I see generations
perpetuating anger.

Suppose there's no death suppose consciousness
Continuously cycles in lifetimes
Meandering in a loopy sort of
Way while the attributes you think

Are so quintessentially you such as
The shapeliness of your body such as the
Suppleness of your mind such as your face
In the mirror are recycled in the

Round do you think your personality
Would persist or is it possible that
Your consciousness and your eyesight
Would be adapting to a different world

With a novel set of inclinations
Or would you face the same old conundrums?

Speculation is
amusing but has limits —
I like ponderous
suppositions but now I
have my chores to finish.

I had a friend who was a poet who
Was terrified by the oblivion
Of space and by Nazi atrociousness
And his fear assumed an angry guise when

Encountering those of lighter views and
He wasn't blaming anyone but he
Believed God was absent and life was cruel
And so he embodied bitterness I

Believe he embraced and he despaired for
Himself for his friends as his mind was a
Whirlpool sinking to a void but as for
Me I suppose we're spirits persisting

In eternity and we have questions
To address and choices to determine.

I see
I question
the birthing of
my eyesight
my questioning.

Temple Eihei-ji

What could a Japanese temple on a
Mountain built in the thirteenth century
Have to do with me — and in ignorance
I lived at the mountain's base and I would

Climb for exercise following a worn
Trail but only on the last day did I
Find the temple entrance — the monk Dogen
Returned from China with empty hands and

The *dharma* and he chose the mountaintop
As a sanctuary and he filled a
Room with candlelight and ever since then
Candles and the *dharma* have been burning —

In America we have the light too
Because Dogen transmitted the knowledge.

So nonsensical
so initially absurd —
what's there to gain by
sitting silently for hours —
there's really nothing to gain.

"Life of Pi"

As yellow staring eyes transfix the goat
It becomes arrow straight and its shoulders
And hips move not very noticeably
In the line of advance the tiger comes

Directly forward moving purposefully
Carefully slowly placing its paws
In a rhythm of attack low to the
Floor and paralyzing the goat the tiger

Comes with its yellow staring eyes and its
Open mouth and its fangs and its stripes it's
Mesmerizing and alarming in waves
The tethered bleating goat knowing there's no

Escaping — the tiger snaps the goat's neck
And drags it along the length of the cage.

In the movie a
father who manages a
zoo showed his son a
tiger is not a thing that
thinks like us — it's not a friend.

Temple Wat Pha Luang

In Thailand poachers killed the adults and
The villagers didn't know what to do
With the tiger cubs so they took them to
A Buddhist temple for the monks to take

Care of and because they're given only
Cooked meat they don't acquire a taste for blood
And so the temple's become a home to
A procession of tigers and monks who

Mingle as if the imperatives of
Violence would disintegrate before
Loving kindness as if benevolence
And compassion were persuasive as if

Buddhism had impetus to turn the
Primordial to a gentle tiger.

So evidently
evolutionary fact
is not conclusive
and a tigerish impulse
can be overcome with love.

Nothing is like an onrushing cold for
Grabbing attention as I felt it in
My throat in my voice when I tried to speak
Especially in my nose which began

To run and mostly in my noggin which
Became seasick and then there were the times
When I rose from bed once the congestion
Had taken hold and my back and shoulders

Felt sore my head throbbed as I went to the
Rest room but there is a lighter side to
Getting sick as it took me out of my
Daily routine separating me from

The hamster wheel of doing the same things
Day after day exertion without thought.

Recovery's not
quite like returning from a
vacation but it
is a rediscovery
of marvelous energy.

I can find a sense of solemnity
Without being a sour puss if I
Recognize the consequences of my
Thoughts and words with people as I often

Underestimate how easily an
Unappealing attitude becomes known
By the slightest gestures of my body
As I am a transmitter of moods and

A recipient of the subtlest
Messages and if I'm kind harmony
Manifests and if grumpy obstacles
Appear as there's a sacred quality

To human interaction as we do
Impact each other for better or worse.

Without intention
my face reveals secrets
without reflection
I don't know what I'm doing —
communication happens.

What is there in a name as I think of
You and your parents at your christening
As they gave you a lovely name in a
Traditional ceremony as a

Bestowal of their best intentions for
You as if they could be present smoothing
Your passage in a life that could involve
Precarious episodes as if they

Could enfold you within the love of Christ
By simply selecting "Kristine" as if
The repetition of your name might serve
As an incantation that would impart

Magical protection throughout your life
Because they won't be with you forever.

A name is a gift
and a reflection of your
parents' desires —
they wished you inspiration
encompassing a lifetime.

There's a rhythm to a running printing
Press and once the settings are right and the
Rollers are inked the paper's loaded and
The copy's been transformed into a plate

And fitted to the roller I can turn
The switch to see the paper raised and fed
And dropped at the other end and then the
Fun begins as adjustments are made and

The image must be good and it takes a
Practiced eye and a head full of knowledge
To a keep a press producing wonderful
Product as chemicals are managed and

Machinery is maintained and the ink
And the water must flow separately.

It looks so easy
as a skilled pressman does it
as nothing goes wrong
but watch as the novice tries —
he gets smeared in printer's ink.

Who cares about compassion anyway?
In our culture it's more important to
Be right to be a leader to get things
Done and the word sounds wimpy so perhaps

It's a concern of women or clergy
But I've discovered as I care about
Myself as I have a family and
Value harmony and happiness for

My children one doesn't incorporate
Difficulties or turn from selfishness
Without understanding the suffering
Of other people and desiring

It's relief and sometimes while I'm feeling
Angry it's helpful to behave kindly.

As a child will rage
an adult could also rage
but it's much better
to turn the energy of
anger to useful purpose.

There's a division between having the
Diabetes and cancer and watching
While healthy as the misfortunes arise
Becoming too much for one to bear and

Witnessing and participating in
Suffering breaks down the dividing lines
Between us as imagination leads
To empathy leads to compassion and

Starting with a loved one understanding
Expands encompassing many and when
I discover the subtle gradations
Of dissatisfaction I realize

Everyone suffers together more or
Less and together we experience.

I was afflicted
with aggressive uniqueness
but bearing witness
helped me to understand
suffering is communal.

It's hard to get the words outside
My mouth because the aggravation builds
To belligerency and while I know
Enough not to trust my inclinations

To see the high and the low responses
Possible it's difficult to take the
Blame in a partnership that's not working
And parsing a litany of events

With an eye for justification in
Defense is not what I want to do and
From experience I know defending
Or attacking is useless and so I

Need to walk away and take the time to
Decompress to locate a friend and talk.

The rollercoaster
of entangled emotions
I've discovered takes
its time to run its course and
later normalcy returns.

Supposedly a dog's nose is hundreds
Of times better than ours and when looking
About I see the people who've mastered
Their dogs walking together side by side

While other pairs aren't so harmonious
And I wonder how the walk would go with
The dog in charge because he's not wedded
To straight lines going from here to there he's

Nosing the delectable enticements
Of the earth and we're oblivious and
We require such pitiful restraint of
Our creatures — how well would you do if we

Put a leash on you and dangled tempting
Aromas out of reach and marched on home?

Are we really the
bestest of friends or are we
ignominious
and parsimonious as our
doggies obey commandments?

A milky sky with the trees coated with
Just fallen snow is a perishable
Wonderland of an hour's duration as
The forecast temperature will reach the

Forties by afternoon as a clipper
Has passed and rain is coming but for now
I'm savoring a moment's interlude
Where the tiny apple tree the pines and

The towering cottonwood are covered
In powered sugar and the sparrow can't
Determine where to land and a squirrel's
Hop-running on the snow and there's not a

Shadow to be seen while everything is
Concealed in a blanket of glowing snow.

As I'm watching the
snow frosting is vanishing
from the limbs and twigs
of the trees and the landscape
is increasingly soggy.

Enso

A child could do it with as much pleasure
As a master with a simple motion
Of the arm holding a brush full of ink
And creating a circle on paper

And the master would know how much ink to
Use would be familiar with the motion
And would have ways of considering the
Child doesn't but in either case making

An enso is an act of creation
As the image represents the motion
Of planets the repetition of the
Seasons the circularity of life

And a child should have the experience
Of exploring with resonate symbols.

That the sun and moon
reappear everyday that
summer becomes fall
that thoughts are repetitive
points to circularity.

Once I was the planet circling you
But now I'm the sun propelling you as
I have acquired the weight and the pull
As I have watched my emotions and have

Learned to let them go as I have practiced
Loving kindness by disbelieving the
Critical mind by not opposing sharp
Thoughts but by observing and by letting them

Go as I have come not to disparage
Myself love arises naturally
And love overcomes separateness and
Love emanates outwards naturally

As light does and without intention I
Have acquired the gravity and poise.

It's not a question
of power or intention
it's the way things are
as love and light emanate
outward and acquire weight.

Think of what I could do with my fingers
As I have known a big guy with large hands
Who was capable of such delicate
Work with wood and I remember my dad

Playing the piano for hours as a
Way of engaging equanimity
And think of the type of spirit I am
To be given the tips of my fingers

For touching and the grip of my hands for
Lifting and the palms for holding that serve
As an extension of my mind that I
May explore the world and fashion a way

Of living harmonious with my thoughts
That I may handle my pressing desires.

Because my fingers
and my mind are passages
to a world filled with
possibilities that I
touch with precision and care.

Even clouds are racing as they've broken
In chunks and are chasing each other and
Even without their leaves the trees in the
Onslaught are roaring and even trunks of

The thin trees are swaying as if they were
Branches and everywhere I turn every
Tree is tossing every bush is moving
A newspaper is flying and the clouds

Are passing and their shadows are moving
But clarity brightens again with the
Sun and I have to turn my back on the
Chilly chafing blowing and I have to

Work hard to keep my balance and every
Second seems approaching a crescendo.

The snow is gone and
the landscape is barren of
growth and it appears
the wind is combing the earth
and winter is vanishing.

If I were discovering my body
As I was growing I'd jump onto the
Top of the refrigerator too and
Just for fun I might push the boxes of

Cereal off to watch them fall and hear
Them plop on the floor and thus to measure
Distance and then I'd gallop joyously
Around the rooms just because I could and

I'd strut out on the narrow ledge and knock
The knick-knacks down one-by-one just to see
Them go and I'd be curious about
The human and the funny noises and

The motions she's making with her arms and
I'd flop on my back and ask to be rubbed.

It's necessary
to be emphatic to be
noisy and grandma
isn't enough to impose
her will on the new kitten.

There are the buds appearing again on
The tips of the trees after a season
Of bareness and the growing insistence
Of the sun that is glaring is like a

Bolt from the sky that's impossible to
Ignore and I'm struck by the potency and
Persistence of the sun turning again
The wheel of the seasons to the time of

Growth and splendor and I am grateful for
The simplicity of its power that
It pours its light on the earth and the grass
Grows the trees bud and the air warms as

It does every spring and I welcome the
Return of the prominence of the light.

There was a moment
of splendor in the winter
when the shine of the
sun shone on the crystals of
the snow and pointed the light.

***Crazy* —**

Where would I be without my sight and my
Hearing and how would I move without my
Arms and legs and what would I be thinking
Without my mind and would I be happy?

If I weren't here to experience my
Being where would I be and also if
This universe weren't here what would be and
What would nothing look like if no one were

Here to see? Does my heart beat itself or
Do I beat it and also does the sun
Burn itself and if not who does? Today
I'm happy to be alive and perhaps

I've been alive a millions times before
But I'm just not able to remember.

If I weren't here would
the earth be here without me
or does my presence
include the earth and the sun
as we create each other?

As ordinary as a squirrel as
Common as a sparrow as everyday
As a gust of wind moving the needles
Of a pine tree the world it seems wiggles

And the quiescence of the apple tree
The rose and the lilac bushes is an
Illusion as they're responding to a
More assertive sun and are preparing

Blossoms — this is where I want to be in
The morning drinking in the barest sights
And sounds because I've come to take pleasure
By noticing how a steady wind stirs

The branches of the maple the walnut
And the cottonwood and I don't need more.

My eyes touch the sun
and the sun embraces me
my ears hold the wind
and the wind caresses me
and we exist together.

Sometimes in idleness I find myself
Entering the labyrinth of my mind
Ruminating on the friendships that went
Wrong and retracing the particulars

Retelling myself the same purposeless
Stories and feeling again emotions
With no resolution and as I have
Done my praying and the amending of

Myself necessary I believe that
The arrival of forgiveness and of
Letting go isn't entirely up
To me and that ruminating with some

Sympathy and humor can be helpful —
After all these years I can be childish.

My ego cherishes
its frustrations and enjoys
replaying stories
for no useful purpose just
to create some excitement.

I wasn't there as I usually
Was when it happened I didn't hear the
Terrific bang but I saw the heavy
Cutting machine knocked into the printing

Press and the double doors bashed apart and
The tool chest askew and the bits of glass
And sheet rock everywhere and I saw the
Van where it shouldn't be in the printing

Room as Dad had lost control of the brake
And couldn't stop in the garage but smashed
The doors in for the second time within
A year but I did see him crestfallen

And tearful as he did acknowledge the
Time had come when he could no longer drive.

We were worried and
sad because he admitted
he was forgetting
his way on the city streets
he's been driving forty years.

The whole expanse of the blue sky mixes
With the trees in the park where the people
Come for these few days of the season as
This is the time of the cherry blossoms —

It's the singularity of the pink
Flowering that touches the heart with a
Color that points the year because now is
When we celebrate the lifting of the

Winter cold and the returning of warm
Breezes and the stirring of growth with a
Strengthening sun and it's natural to
Rejoice and cherish the moment of the

Cherry blooms because it may rain and the
Blossoms may separate and so vanish.

It's quite natural
when the sun strengthens again
for people to rejoice and
create a ceremony.

The blooming crabapple tree is peaking
And its blossoms are streaming in the wind
While other flowering trees and hedges
Are opening and creating such a

Captivating sight as I'm driving in
Town and I'm wondering why this slice of
Nature affects me so as mosquitoes
And wood ticks are as natural as the

Cherry blooms as common as a bout of
Frenzied thinking my mind endures and so
Maybe it's better not to question but
To appreciate the periodic

Appearance of beauty on the earth as
It blooms and then vanishes in the wind.

I can do without
the mosquitoes and wood ticks
but it is my choice
to overlook the pests and
be enamored with beauty.

That before my eyes the squirrel would run
The length of the top of the long white fence
Without stopping — and the robin would stop
In the apple tree for a brief rest and

Then fly — that the leaves are half-way growing
And the grass is rising up and the sky
Is sunny but was rainy yesterday —
And my eyes are seeing and my mind is

Absorbing the scene without distraction —
As I'm indulging the freedom to see
The thinnest of clouds disintegrating —
And I remember other seasons of

My living when I was lost in yearnings
And dissatisfactions and now I'm not.

I am the center
of my being and I may
direct attention
in whatever direction
suits me within the moment.

I gaze at the perpetrator in the
Mirror every morning and start with the
Left side of my chin with downward strokes and
Then I go under my nose and it does

Become apparent when it's time to change
The razor because a dull blade will drag
Above my lip where I am sensitive —
I could be thinking about politics

Or the Academy Awards — while on
My right side next to my ear I begin
Stroking down against the grain to my neck
Until I reach my chin and when finished

I like to put the razor down and with
My fingers I like to feel smoothiness.

I've just discovered
an oddity that's
taken forever
to notice — my right
side is hairier.

Sadly a sense of dignity comes and
Eliminates possibilities so
Adults really can't descend again to
The excitements and pleasures of childhood

Because what would it look like to see the
Usual person of middle-age girth
On the monkey bars at the playground and
Can you imagine a husband and wife

On the titter totter or a man of
Business on the merry-go-round so no
It's OK to watch the kids or grandkids
Who don't have a thought about how they look

Who think its funny to get dizzy or
Silly but adults must be dignified.

So what's up with the
water-skiers and surfers
bungee-cord jumpers
the hikers and skydivers —
what's with the rollercoaster?

I want to be left alone thank you I
Sometimes think to myself especially
When focusing on the radio or
A task as I have expectations of

People for the things I want them to do
For me and ordinarily there's the
Give and take of cooking and cleaning and
Mowing the grass and paying bills that are

Obvious but there's also a subtle
Measuring of emotional service
Whether I'm receiving what's due me and
It is probable I don't even know

The demands I'm making on those I love
Because I don't see my expectations.

And it's funny how
needy I can be without
knowing it and it's
so funny what everyone
expects without saying so.

My mind today is predominately
A grayish sky the rain is falling from
But I'm not unhappy I'm savoring
A chilly day in a warming season

A burst of rain followed by quietness
The leaves growing to fullness and not yet
Nibbled by the insects and I do take
Pleasure in each of three shades of lilac

Blossoms in the hedge that I planted so
Many years ago and don't remember
Noticing before now and noticing
Is the trick I've learned during a season

Of living that rain or shine whatever
I'm right on the edge of transformation.

I'm not separate
from anything I see I'm
predominately
a vessel of sensations
navigating mystery.

Roses in poetry have become trite
As everyone has written of the folds
Within folds within folds and contrasted
Petals with thorns as if the beauty and

The sharpness had a point but during most
Of the year the rose bush consists of stems
And little leaves and yes the bloom in spring
Is lovely emerging in a shower

Of sunlight within a season bursting
With growth and for some reason poets do
Keep writing about roses — more so than
Chrysanthemums — as if a rose were a

Sight to behold like the sun and the moon
And in beholding a rose I am caught.

So there is something
about the bloom of a rose
like the sun and moon
captivating enchanting
eyes capable of seeing.

I'm lucky I've heard anger is a form
Of suffering as it's necessary
To stand apart and watch it's effects to
See destructive qualities — I'm lucky

To be with a group that values kindness
Because cherishing hatreds together
Against opposing groups could override
My capacity for careful thinking —

As anger fixes on a target and
Burns the heart and the intellect will find
Justifications and who hasn't known
Justifiable anger and villains

But not enough people recognize how
Blinding obsessive anger can become.

I know it's my job
to experience anger
to suffer anger
enough to desire a
more careful way to live.

A stone a rose and an apple appear and
The stone fits within my palm weighty and
Smooth with curving contours and a flatter
Side minutely pitted and the petals

Of the yellow rose are silky between
My fingers and the tip of a thorn is
Sharp on my thumb and I gaze at the folds
In folds in folds of the blossom and the

Apple is red and yellow and the skin
Is crisp and the fruit is tasty and I
Take a bite as big as I can manage
And discover I'm quite hungry and just

These simple pastimes are enough for now —
I don't have to let my mind cogitate.

Sometimes I love to
touch the surface of a stone
see the rose's bloom
eat an entire apple
return to simplicity.

Monkey Mind

His guru had one more suggestion as
He was leaving saying "one thing you must not
Do when meditating this week think about
Monkeys" and how easy thought the student

As these creatures never crossed his mind but
This week while sitting his thoughts exploded
With somber gorillas toothy baboons
Monkeys with red bottoms and rambunctious

Scampering chattering even shrieking
Chimpanzees and he was angry with his
Master saying "You did this purposely
Your instructions not to think about them

Made it likely I would think about them"
And smiling the guru said "now you see."

And so with any
difficulty trying to
escape certain thoughts
doesn't make them go away
but only makes them stronger.

Matt's a six-foot banana today on
The sidewalk and might have been Gumby a
Coke bottle or Spiderman yesterday
And he's standing and driving a Segway

A T-shaped vehicle with two wheels and
He was a soldier in Afghanistan
Was shot in the head has memory loss
And headaches and because he can't work he

Passes the time in a costume looking
Ridiculous to snare the attention
Of passersby attempting to impart
Happiness because he intends to turn

Around a bad day someone is having
Because his humor is the best of him.

It's too easy
to become isolated
laughter is magic
humor communicates and
people need inspiration.

I liked the upright posture of the seat
Because I stayed alert while driving and
It's smallness made turning zippy and the
Compact windshield was right-sized and over

The years it became such a familiar
Pleasure as natural as putting on
A jacket and going anywhere as
Easily as walking and the trips my

Family took the daily motion of
My life adhered to the PT Cruiser
So when the electronics failed the cost
Of its repair soared reluctantly I

Decided to trade it for whatever
I could — I turned my back and walked away.

Things I've acquired
are material objects
tools of convenience
but my enthusiasm
encompasses everything.

Hot Wheels

As a child I loved toys especially
Collectables and I gathered dozens
Of small cars with pin axels allowing
Their wheels to spin easily and each was

Precious and when I see a specific
Shade of yellow I yearn for one of my
Lost possessions but at the Toyota
Dealership I could only choose one so

I chose a Corolla because I love
It's size style and reputed quality
And I wavered between a choice of black
Or red and was partly determined by

The newer tires on the one I bought but
I was captivated by its candy red.

Do I possess the
car or does it possess me?
Could I do without
possessions or am I a
captive of collectables?

I see how Bill Elliot's converted
The gas station on the corner into a
Two-story home with a stairway to
The roof and a railing on the top for

Gazing about when the warmth returns and
Sometimes he meanders around without
A shirt exhibiting his extra pounds
His ponytail with nonchalance and with

Apparent leisure and I do admire
His decoration of the waist-high wrought
Iron fence with blue green silver and red
Pinwheels because he's perceptive because

The spinning wheels in spring are becoming
Because they do complement the blossoms.

Disregarding the
conventional taking
different paths and
using imagination
is the American dream.

In Stillwater

While I'm sitting on a wall designed to
Hold a river rising with the flood of
Springtime I'm seeing the distance to the
Limestone bluffs on the other side of the

Valley watching as the undulating
Water on the surface sparkles in waves
Disconnected from the direction of
What must be a massive current moving

To an ocean and I'm allowing my
Mind to settle with the tiny waves as
If the movement and my thoughts were one thing
For the time being with the sun on my

Face and then I realize how much like
The water I am always in motion.

As my thoughts are
settling and my blood is
circulating and
my heart is beating I'm not
even lifting a finger.

The accelerator and the steering
Are automatic — the four lanes and the
Sparse traffic are perfect for swift passage
Over the rolling hills of Wisconsin

Under a sky dotted all the way to
The horizon with clouds — and farms and trees
Arise flowing indistinguishably
In a vast and constant procession and

I'm consuming distance by watching the
Mammoth trucks I pass and by seeing a
Singularly tall hill that's twenty miles
Ahead that is surprisingly modest

As it vanishes off to my right and
Becomes predictably forgettable.

In a tangle of
construction in Green Bay
I missed a turn and
consternation swearing and
sweat predominated.

The Trick

Don't be hypnotized by these words because
This poem is a manipulation
And the letters and the syllables were
Measured for the creation of cadence

Selected for the accentuation
Of sounds pleasing both the ears and eyes as
You may read or hear these lines and each word
Carries only an approximation

Of meaning and the words aren't true but
They point to a reality beyond words —
I take the time in the morning to touch
The sunrise with my eyes and the rising

Sun dissolves the tensions of yesterday
And I'm titillated with its beauty.

The waves of sunlight
bedazzle my senses and
just for a moment
this ordinary morning
is extraordinary.

The retaining wall was bulging and would
Not have stood another season so we
Disassembled blocks put aside busted
Pieces and shoveled a new foundation

And we carved into the bank — making a
Pile of dirt — and we spread pea gravel to
Establish a level base and stretched a
Taut line for guidance and as the sun blazed

We placed new blocks of a sturdier type
Below and replaced the undamaged blocks
Layer on layer and for fill behind
The wall we dumped pea gravel and broken

Stone with the intention that water would
Pass between the fill and blocks harmlessly.

The neighbor wanted
the extra dirt and we used
her mini-tractor
and a trailer shoveling
it in and spreading it out.

Poetics

Aristotle supposed that music has
A civilizing or a barbarous
Influence and who would argue the point
That listening to a symphony in

A hall designed for resonance doesn't
Impart refinement but such wasn't the
Setting I encountered last night with the
Pulsating syrupy blues playing good

And loud and there I sat struggling with
The urge and embarrassment of looking
Foolish that I overcame to become
Again the whirling dervish of thirty

Years ago as the music took me from
 Self-consciousness to such joy in motion.

Taken completely
with raw pulsating rhythm
without melody
I simply became music
without a care in my head.

There's nothing selfish about it and it's
Necessary to practice ignoring
My nagging conscience saying I should be
Sad because you're sad or share your anger

With someone else and when I've done something
To precipitate your anger I catch
Myself becoming angry denying
Blame and feeling guilty too because I

Have no surety for judging so I
Breathe calming breaths and become a little
Distant from you perhaps leaving the room
Because I want to be the captain of

My emotions in a ship with enough
Ballast to weather the difficult seas.

It's not possible
to be compassionate if
I'm just reacting
so I really do need to
discover my surety.

Just for today I am the breeze in the
Trees I am the sound of peace and I am
Breath visible in the leaves and I am
A sparrow on a twig for a moment

And just for today I am the warm sun
On the skin of my legs and I am the
Clarity of light in the valley and
I am the glimmer and sparkle of the

Sun on the river and just for today
I am undulating water I am
The sounds of the cars rising in the
Air in the city I am the faces

And the voices of the people passing
By on the street just for today I am.

I am forgetful
I am forgiveness today
I am the morning
I am the moment without
anticipation or fear.

Impetuosity is a spaniel
Bounding and turning in the grass without
Hesitation as he's free to roam and
Romp and lunge and dart and taste and smell to

Satisfaction until he's exhausted
With exuberance and what a joy it
Is to watch such rollicking expression
With a tinge perhaps of envy as I

Recognize if I behaved that way they'd
Lock me up and anyway I've acquired
Prohibitions and inhibitions and
My appearance needs consideration

And I have consequences to beware —
I've lost the innocence of ignorance.

My inner spaniel
talks and laughs and reads and writes
and exercises
I'm free to roam and to romp
and to write any damn thing.

As the years are accumulating the
Seasons are becoming precious to me
And in the transition from winter I
Watched the tips of trees begin to bud

And noticed the vulnerability
And the beseeching posture of the limbs
Rising up to the sun but now in the
Summer their forms are concealed within

Luxuriant foliage and I'm attuned
To the ascending and dissipating
Sound of the wind in the leaves just as if
The trees are sighing and I remember

These voices from childhood resonating
Communicating succoring soothing.

The invisible
undulating in the trees
the inaudible
arising within the leaves
communicating soothing.

Proximity

As if my thoughts were secrets only I
Should know as if my secrets were precious
Separating you from me defining
Our differences establishing borders

But it doesn't matter that I'm quiet
And you're boisterous I'm doubtful and you're
Confident that people come to you and
I'm often alone because I am not

Alone and though I choose to be quiet
And separate my thoughts and emotions
Are communal and secrets meaningless —
A person lives with the nourishment of

Love and dies in isolation and so
I have to practice communication.

No one lives alone
separateness is deadly
and to be happy
I have to discover how
to communicate with you.

A weighty can of peaches fell from the
Shelf and broke her toe and she was angry
With me because I put it up where it
Could fall and yes I knew the door of the

Closet's sticky and needs a determined
Jerk but I couldn't have known her hefty
Yank would agitate the peaches and break
Her toe but it did and I'm familiar

With the fun of reactionary rage
And I could've become angry too but
For some reason that day I didn't and
Discovered I don't have to play the game

It's not necessary to react with
Anger and I'm quite capable of poise.

While I'm not happy
the peaches broke her toe I'll
remember the day
when I could've been angry
but instead learned to be kind.

After an hour of sleep I woke to hear
The minutest whine of a mosquito
Just about my ear so I took a swipe
But missed and slapped my ear instead and then

I lay awake listening and hearing it
Coming near and going away and I
Almost fell asleep again but there it
Was and I slapped my ear again and missed

So I turned on the lights and looked about
Determined for blood but as it was the
Smallest mosquito it couldn't be seen
So I lay in bed listening breathing

On the verge of sleep and jolting awake
Because of this tiniest irritant.

This morning is the
clearest and deepest kind of
blue sky but I am
woozy and wondering why
we must have mosquitoes.

.

I'm not over it yet and there's no use
Pretending I am as I think about
The way you seduced me by being coy
And vulnerable and asking for my

Help appealing to my libido as
Much as my vanity and ignorance
As you are perceptive and skilled and yet
I'm grateful for the discoveries you

Generated that love and passion are
Different — passion is a great force and
Love is a need for the deepest sharing
And passion is addictive while love is

A calling a metamorphosis and
I discovered how to love selflessly.

I gave away
my secrets and desires
you knew my thoughts and
though you weren't trustworthy
I learned to share everything.

The torque of its motor is impressive
In the morning darkness as I'm in bed
As the rumbling behemoth arrives
And stops and as a mechanical whine

Begins as I know its arm is clamping
The container and lifting as I hear
Clinking clunking rattling evidence
Of trash settling on trash and then I

Hear the whine and then the rumbling as
The leviathan departs with its so
Odiferous cargo supplemented
With my modest offerings and I think

How wonderful it is at my leisure
To be observing civilization.

We each have a role
and we acquire the most
exquisite talents
with such specialized tools all
for the benefit of all.

I had to remind myself as I was
Lying on my side with my elbow bent
Above my head for a very long hour
That this was a voluntary ordeal

And the application of the thickest
Needles for outlining was the most
Excruciating and I doubted I could
Stand it but once the job's begun there's no

Turning back so I reminded myself
I adored the peacock feather as a
Symbol worthy of intimacy so
I shut my eyes and endured the needles —

Tattooing on the ribs is tortuous
But not torture if you're asking for it.

Usually it's
over when it's over but
I had determined
to return the following
day to do the other side.

Youth and ignorance aren't an advantage
For selecting the first tattoo because
Without experience there's no context
For judging and in my case I became

Excited and decided without much
Thinking and so in Galveston Texas
Harpoon Barry incised an odious
Swallow on my chest I wore shamefully

But a tattoo should inspire with a
Resonant meaning and beforehand it
Should be visualized precisely where
It's to be and the artist shouldn't be

Any stray dog but should be respected
With a portfolio of work to show.

The embarrassing
swallow was majestically
overlaid with an
eagle in a flurry and
a festival of motion.

Even on a cloudy day in summer
There is radiance penetrating as
I go about my life inattentive of
Its presence sustaining me even as

The rain is falling in sheets and water
Is flowing on the streets on the way to
The river there is radiance moving
Ceaselessly nourishing me even in

The middle of the night as I'm dreaming
Under a panorama of stars and
A half moon there is unsurpassable
Radiance coursing in my veins and in

The morning the sun rises again to
Compose the day with brilliant energy

The enveloping
animating radiance
of the weighty sun
is ceaselessly burning and
showering the earth with life.

Because water flows from high to low and
Because the water happened to flow in
Arizona in one direction the
Canyons were carved for thousands of years and

To me they appear beautiful but when
The pressure accumulates along the
Fault lines of the Earth's crust and suddenly
There's a break underwater and a surge

Of the ocean overwhelms a coastal
Village in Japan and people and homes
Are caught in a wall of water and swept
Out to sea as the water returns

To me it's horrible to be against
Unpredictable all consuming force.

There's not a hint of
of the precariousness
of life or of the
massive power of water
in a single drifting cloud.
.

With a red nose and watery eyes with
A hazy dizziness in the way of
Easy thought I endured forty summers
Of allergic frustration and though I

Didn't die and compensated with a
Plethora of handkerchiefs I would have
Eagerly traded noses but then a
Clever specialist spotted the polyps

In my nasal cavities and he zapped them
With steroids and now my daily sprays
Are working and I may go anywhere
With a dry nose and a clear head and with

Eyes liberated but sometimes I
Regret the time saturated with sneezes.

I could've been an
intellectual or a
foolish romantic
could've traveled anywhere —
I could've been a hero.

The apex of the summer is passing
The power of the sun is lessening
The light is becoming golden gilding
The leaves and the grass — and the air is a

Medley of cool and warm — and in the late
Afternoon though the sun may swelter with
Fierceness it doesn't last long and as the
Sun is setting earlier a chill is

Emerging at night and it's easier
To sleep under covers with the windows
Open with a chorus of crickets in
The breezes and I'm not tossing in bed

In the muggy air because late summer
Is the absolute pinnacle for dreams.

Blue skies arise in
every season but the earth
responds differently
as the sun cooperates
with the earth's revolutions.

The St. Croix Crossing Bridge

For fifty years we've been arguing and
Having lawsuits about spanning the St.
Croix River Valley with a new bridge
And it took a congressional vote and

A president's signature to sweep
Aside opposition and vast swaths of
Earth have been moved and deep piers established
Through the mucky bottom into bedrock

So in the air over a distance a
Steel and concrete form aerodynamic
And graceful has risen representing
A modern monument of beautiful

Lines with utilitarian purpose
And traffic will hum over the valley.

We don't have the time
to dawdle on scenery
we're driven by the
necessity to keep up
with the pace of our email.

Trilling far off and throbbing nearby the
Crickets are blanketing the darkness with
Sound and if I were slumbering wouldn't
They be whispering messages of peace

And wouldn't I have forgotten worries
And wouldn't I be with my companions
And perhaps the rhythm of the crickets
Would become music and celebration

But I can't escape nervousness and my
Thoughts are churning uselessly and my
Eyes are burning holes in the night but as
Weary as I am I return again

And again to the evidence of the
Crickets — there's really no need to worry.

On the edge of sleep
I don't care where I am or
struggle with problems
because I'm traveling and
don't even know who I am.

In the middle of August while driving
In Stillwater I notice the tips of
The leaves are coloring as I'm wearing
A t-shirt and don't remember when the

Seasons usually turn and because
It's muggy this afternoon it's hard to
Imagine snow — but on the driveway I
See a red maple leaf and realize

Summer doesn't last — so I look for the
Tree and become familiar again with
The neighborhood and find the maple and
See a sprinkling of red at the top

And remember this tree every autumn
Becomes the epitome of crimson.

I remember the
the maple trees in Kyoto
grow miniature leaves
that present the perfection
of autumn crimson brilliance.

When we moved in twenty years ago there
Were fleas to exterminate and water
Was seeping into the basement but there
Was a furnace a washer a dryer

And a refrigerator and over
Years we tore out carpet re-shingled the
Roof replaced the water heater and the
Roots of the cottonwood tree busted the

Sewage pipe costing thousands of dollars
To repair while I've been watching as the
Kids got taller and outgrew taking the
Bus to school and came home on holidays

From college and while they've moved away the
Structure of home contains the memories.

It's easy to
dry-vac basement
water but as
the driveway wears
puddles get bigger.

Avalokiteshvara

The one comprehending the suffering
Of everyone having a thousand eyes
And hands who is compassionate who is
Moved to alleviate the suffering

Of so much and so many such a one
Would be invisibly and ceaselessly
Acting everywhere within and without —
While I understand so little of the

Suffering I inflame of myself and
Others while in agitation I ask
Why in the world the bodhisattva is
Necessary while I resist coming

To embody compassion myself how
Is liberation even possible?

I believe in
simplicity
sincerity
and want to be
compassionate.

As if it were an emissary from
Paradise the peacock arises in
This world where people suffer accidents
Disease violence where the spirit is

Vulnerable to pain exhaustion and
Depression it comes with opalescent
Green and blue and bronze it promenades with
A fan of voluptuous feathers each

With a regal core of purple and how
Do we reconcile inescapable
Difficulty with inexplicable
Beauty except to believe there is more

To living than we can appreciate
And the peacock is a hint of marvels.

Like children see
the beauty of the peacock
the bloom of the rose
the majesty of mountains
the splendor of sunrises.

It is possible to take pleasure in
The everyday experience of the
Sun — but while driving I was listening
To commentary on the radio

About a celebrity who was at
A restaurant having lunch and because
The politics of the famous diner
Were prominent and controversial

A server doused the diner with a glass
Of water and the personalities
On the radio were offended by
The praise the server was enjoying on

Snapchat on Twitter and on Facebook —
Gleeful virtuous congratulations.

My mind is a bowl
open to cottonwood leaves
dancing in a breeze
but now I am distracted
and sunlight is out of reach.

The silhouette of me on the sidewalk
Walking ahead synchronized perfectly
With every motion of my body is
Spooky as I'm seeing my shadow self

As a symbol not of who I am now
But of whom I previously could have
Been in other lifetimes or of whom I
Could become if I let myself go far

Enough because I'm a dynamo of
Elasticity and when driven by
Drug addiction I trespassed boundaries
I never expected to cross and in

Recovery I discovered I am
Capable of genuine compassion.

I am a walking
potentiality for
better or worse or
an indifferent mixture
depending on my choices.

We go to the sanctuary of the
Church early in the morning just as the
Sun is lighting the stained glass windows and
We practice walking meditation by

Ceaselessly carefully taking small steps
Following each other in silence and
Synchronizing our steps and breaths as well
As possible mixing Zen within a

Setting of Christian artistry with the
Intention of sharing the moment with
Settled minds and simple motion and the
Quiet presence in the sanctuary

Reminds me I don't have to hurry and
It's quite possible to embody peace.

The green blue red gold
Purple and yellow of the
Stained glass windows are
Variously dim or bright
Depending on the season.

As we do our walking meditation
In the sanctuary of the church we
Try to synchronize our steps and breaths with
Each other to achieve harmony and

Simplicity and openness and I
See a stained glass window with an ark and
A dove curving vines and leaves illumined
By the rising sun and there's a plaque of

Dedication to Tom Phillips — who was
Pastor of the church — to his wife Percy —
And I recall his persistent kindness
And his quiet watchfulness in this place

And I realize stepping carefully
Is exerting comforting influence.

The memorials
are visible reminders
designed for seeing
and perpetuating love
but memory perishes.

I'm ambivalent about having a
Memory as it's loaded with regrets
And wounds and also victories that I've
Transformed to triumphs I use to measure

Myself against others and the past is
Filtered through my story-telling machine
Because I want to ascribe meaning to
Events because I do need a sense of

Direction but how I determine to
Remember a friendship that dissolved and
Hurt is paramount because it's easy
To be a victim nourishing anger

Preventing spontaneous forgiveness
And making compassion impossible.

I do remember
as I choose to remember
and my choices are
determinate so I need
to practice circumspection.

The Mirror

It's just glass with a solid backing yet
It's acquired magical quality
Reflecting perfectly anyone who
Comes before it so what is its value

In an empty room with no one looking
As it's like a box without a lid as
It's not complete without a consciousness
Apprehending its visions and we who

Come before it should beware because it
Casts a spell by implying the image
Is the self when really it's the ego
Seeing the ego evaluating

Cherishing or disparaging so we
Go away deluded about ourselves.

Imagine living
without knowing how you look
how differently would
you think about yourself and
is it even possible?

The Person in the Mirror

Imagine yourself on a journey of
Consecutive lifetimes and with every
Birth comes different parents and siblings
And economic circumstances and

Alternating genders and a new face
And differences in strength and health and in
Grace of body and acuity of
Mind and in each instance you adapt

As well as you may with gathered or with
Dissipated confidence perceiving
Either oppression or well being and
Desiring accomplishment and praise

So when you gaze at you in the mirror
Do you recognize basic consciousness?

Suppose death is a
turning of circumstances
a rearrangement
of superficial facts — how
much of you comes with you?

Imagine having coffee with one of
Your friends and the deity played a joke
And transformed both of you so you would be
Looking at your face with your friend's eyes and

Your memory and habits were within
Her body and though the voice expressing
Your surprise would be quite familiar it's
Not what you're used to as it's a woman's

And you were a man — could you go home to
Her family or would you return to your
Wife with her body because how could you
Walk into someone else's life and know

How to behave because more than just a
Body the universe would be scrambled?

Can the body and
consciousness be divided?
Can the universe
that creates incarnation
really be comprehended?

The Way

Do I have the power to be happy
In my ways of relating with people
In my habits within the convergence
Of circumstances when I find myself

Opposed to someone or suffering from
Illness or difficulty how do I
Cope when my choices are complex and fraught
With uncertainty when what I want seems

Unobtainable and what I possess
Unbearable am I able to sleep
In the pivotal periods before
Resolution and do I realize

My eyes aren't unique and everyone more
Or less encounters the dark and the light?

Am I possessed by
my emotions or have I
found the practices
for equanimity and
compassionate engagement?

How could a life be evaluated
Without considering relationships
In marriages and friendships and working
Partnerships because we are designed for

Communication and our different
Talents and often antagonistic
Perspectives do produce society —
It's a mystery to me why the friend

I knew to be available and kind
For twelve years became cold and evasive
Without explanation and I grieve the
Absence of a friend — and I resent the

Presence of the stranger my friend became
Because now I'm missing conversation.

I do create
stories about
failed friendships
and I want to
be big hearted.

The autumn colors are extinguished and
Bare trees are waving in a steady wind
And I remember here in this room my
Dad stumbled backwards hitting his head

On the tile and I lifted from behind
With my arms under his getting him up
Dazed — I don't remember how we got him
To the hospital and it was only

A single event in a series of
Accidents and illnesses marking an
Irreversible decline but very
Often when visiting I saw him propped

Up in different hospital beds cheerful
As if he were taking a vacation.

I remember Dad
in the hospital
hospitable
welcoming
visitors.

The streets are stark again as I'm driving
And seeing the overcast sky through bare
Branches again that arrived yesterday
And there's the carcass of a squirrel on

The road being jabbed by several crows and
And I can't help missing the other birds
And I remember the summer foliage
And I pass the crabapple trees that bloom

In spring — but Thanksgiving is coming soon
And then Christmas and New Year's Day and I
Will take the opportunity to wear
My colorful fleece shirts that I only

Wear in winter and I'm doing my best
To savor diminished sunlight again.

It's a season
of celebrations
of companionship
of expressions of
enthusiasm.

A good home is filled with memories of
Thanksgivings Christmases and Easters when
Everyone gathered to discuss the news
And the feasts were prepared with the skills of

Accumulated years and I never
Really leave but carry the loving through
Life as a foundation to build on but
When I enter in again the chair where

My dad sat the couch where he napped and the
Painting that watched over him are tinged with
Sadness as recollections of his hives
His faintings and his slow decline are now

Inseparable with the fact nothing
Lasts forever not even memory.

In a home every
item carries memories
of its origin
of how it came to its place
and of who would care for it.

This winter I'm seeing the naked trees
And remembering I will be sixty
Years old in November but I'm lucky
Because I don't feel my age and because

Of my exercise I'm as spry as a
Teenager — but I have wrinkles about
My eyes and I have memories also
And as I'm driving and seeing the bare

Branches of the trees overhanging the
Street I remember the cathedrals in
England I saw when I was a student
And realize that the stone tracery

In those churches are meant to represent
The graceful lines of trees in the winter.

I'm sometimes
surprised by
eyesight
memory
and insight.

Asthma

I'm sitting still but chugging right along
Like a company of Greek warriors
Plying their oars in battle because two
Days ago I acquired a cough that

Would not let go and though I go to the
Gym everyday doing cardio work
At night in bed my coughing continued
With equal determination so I

Visited a doctor and he prescribed
Prednisone to fight the inflammation
In my lungs and so the circulation
Of my blood is throbbing as if I were

At the gym on a machine but I'm not
Lifting a finger while smiting the cough.

I imagine the
predicament of having
a persistent cough
while not having a doctor
and not having Prednisone.

I'm grateful for the asphalt because if
My driveway were gravel I'd be blowing
It away bit by bit and I'm happy
To have my sturdy snow blower because

No matter how prodigious the dump it
Plods along spewing the snow to the side
And I can swivel the direction of
The spray by turning a handle because

I don't want to blow into a fierce wind
Because my face would get crusted with the
Snow and as long as the temperature
Stays well below freezing I'll be OK

Because if the snow warms to slushiness
The snow blower clogs and then I shovel.

It's not much fun
thrusting away with
a loaded shovel
with snow sticking
to the metal.

Portrait

She smiles with ease, as lovely as a child;
And like a child she laughs with simple joys,
As though a candle's radiance were wild
Enough and life and love and men were toys.
Her girlish blush is coy and innocent,
Her slender form displays her elegance,
Her shoulder's curve is slim and delicate,
And all her movements sketch a feline grace.
Why does her beauty spark so much unrest?
How may her innocence exact such shame?
When she is near my loneliness has rest,
And love's seduction seems a harmless game.
But she contrives her lovely smile with ease,
And all her dear affections only tease.

— *Tekkan*

Everyday Mind II

Only banana

tastes like banana

only a tongue

can taste banana —

I have the joy.

When the wind blows through the bare branches of
The trees on a morning in December
When there's a chill rising from the snow on
The ground when the sky's predominately

Cloudy with scattered stretches of blue there's
A bleakness about the moment as the
Trees epitomize the absence of the
Sun as in stark nakedness they're swaying

In a fierce wind that's not leavened with the
Soothing sound of the leaves and yet there's a
Warmth in my heart and a kind of austere
Beauty about this day that reminds me the

Sun's not really absent life endures and
I discover fortitude in winter.

Suddenly there's a
Pileated woodpecker
on the cottonwood
Striking the tree with its beak —
its scarlet head is lovely.

I became habituated to the
Timing of your episodes with years of
Experience responding to you and
I anticipated your becoming

Angry again your blaming me again
For incidental matters not worth the
Agitation and I was defensive
And I got angry but gradually

With disciplined intention I got good
At balancing my emotions because
I did from the beginning understand
You inherited generations of

Misery from your family and I fought
With myself and became compassionate.

I didn't become
compassionate by hiding
in safe places I
had to suffer myself
and grow with the suffering.

The daughter of the gambler lives today
In the woman who occasionally
Loses control of her emotions who
Disturbs family holidays who harbors

A burning fuse leading to eruption —
And she's not intending to be angry
And she's not aware of her dynamic
Personality as she's reliving

The days when her father ran off with his
Company's money and lost it betting
On horse races as she's repeatedly
Going through the dissolution of her

Family and the unexplainable
Betrayals feeling abandoned again.

I remind myself
I didn't cause the turmoil
can't cure the turmoil
and can't control the turmoil
but compassion is helpful.

Periphery

I couldn't prosper without my circles
Of friends where I take my place as one of
The whole where I go to mix myself with
Others because I need to know how to

Become useful and what role suits me and
Sometimes words flow out as naturally
As breathing and sometimes I catch myself
Measuring who they are and who I am

And I don't seem able to bridge the gap
And I realize they aren't imposing
The sense of separation I'm feeling —
I'm isolating myself because I'm

In a hole of vulnerability —
But now I know the mood will dissipate.

Rediscovering
the role that suits me within
my circle of friends
is child's play when I forget
who I think I am.

I've gotten a lot of mileage out of
Playing the sleepless poet rummaging
For significance and sacrificing
While everyone else is sleeping and I'm

Stubborn and I'll pay the penalty in
Taxes for not having health coverage
I'll stop taking trazodone my magic
Sleeping pills because I refuse to pay

Hundreds of dollars just to consult the
Doctor once just to update prescriptions
So I went to the pharmacy looking
For non-prescription drugs and I talked to

The pharmacist and he impolitely
Asked me so how much coffee do you drink?

Could it be the pot
of coffee I drink each day
lifting me up in
the morning making me buzz
keeping me awake at night?

It's the irascible caw of the crow
Communicating intelligence and
A warning to trespassers it's not a
Joke to linger in its territory

And I know it's not alone a cohort
Of black eyes are watching from the trees and
If I were small enough the menace of
The caw would be terrifying but as

It is I just register the sound and
Think of its sharp beak and remember crows
Stabbing and cutting carcasses of the
Squirrels and rabbits they didn't kill but

Came upon already dead to feast on
While hopping and watching with piercing eyes.

The menace of its
caw the blunt strength of its beak
the enforcement of
territoriality
make the crow formidable.

Of all the things to do she has chosen
To befriend the crows of the neighborhood
By offering chicken or beef to them
And when she emerges from home there is

Recognition and communication
Welcome anticipation in the trees
For her as a small place has become a
Sanctuary from separateness —

Imaginative curiosity
For a bird people ordinarily
Dislike has moved her to offer the crows
The nurturance every creature needs and

There is no telling how simple goodness
May manifest before it's exercised.

Offering friendship
imaginatively so
respectfully so
to the irascible crows
turned the universe a bit.

I seldom consider the beating of
My heart the circulation of my blood
In my arteries and capillaries
As they nourish my toes and finger tips

Because the pulsation within me is
Spontaneous — and every day while I'm
Walking in the bitter cold of winter
I don't often have a clear sky to see

A golden sun rising and even if
I did I might not notice the sun if
I'm pondering politics because the
Sun comes up consistently — but whether

I'm cognizant or not my life depends
On a beating heart and a rising sun.

The circulation
of blood and the burning of
the sun aren't really
identical energies
but they are simpatico.

George says hello with a quivering chirp
As I'm entering the room and he's
Leaning his head on the piano leg
With his back legs sprawling as lazy as

Possible — a portrait of nonchalance —
He's not a kitten anymore and not
A grown-up either and there's not a thing
He does but eat and sleep but he knows my

Habits during the night and leads me to
The necessary room but he ambles
More slowly than I want to go so I
Slow down because I can't get around him

Because George is large and doesn't hurry
And I'm the one who's being disciplined.

George hasn't a mane
isn't on the savanna
doesn't have a pride
but he is brown and does have
a complacent majesty.

I love the morning sunrise transforming
An open sky and casting a shine on
On the snow covered ground with the squirrel
Tracks and the sides and the roofs of the homes

Brilliant because I love to see clearly
Because my thinking is uncluttered and
A natural optimism rises
As if the frictions and complexities

Of yesterday dissolve in the blue sky
And the renewing power of the sun —
But soon my thoughts will assume the burden
Of problems needing solutions and of

Driving emotions and relationships
As I engage with my difficulties.

As if I'm reborn
by the transforming sunrise
as if I'm a child
again liberated from
problems needing solutions.

There's nothing like sub zero wind sculpting
The snow in curvaceous banks and filling
The air with a mist of snow crystals as
Lacerating wind becomes visible

And after a few days the cars become
Caked with the salt on the roads melting the
Ice but also plastering cars about
The tires with a muck of brown ice and

A few minutes in the cold is enough
To zap my glasses and when I enter
The warmth of the house again my lenses
Immediately crust with fog and it

Takes a marshalling of will to leave home
To do the necessary chores of life.

If I let the car
warm up in the driveway for
five minutes it's
not necessary to scrape
the windshield as the ice melts.

I'm ambivalent about a thawing
After the bitter cold and a weighty
Snowfall because it's not as if spring is
Around the corner — we've got three more months

Of winter and all the warming does is
Create an unavoidable world of
Mucky snow on the sidewalks on the roads
And the cars get smeared with salt and crud and

Nothing is beautiful and everything
Sucks and yet the clouds are glowing in the
Morning light as they so gradually
Transform and if I take the time to see

The resplendence here the gossamer there
It's easy to forget inconvenience.

If it were up to
me the temperature would be
twenty degrees from
December to April and
Someone else would shovel snow.

Routine

When meditating in the morning I
Sit on the edge of emptiness as my
Thinking intervenes — when attending a
Circle of sober alcoholics I

Hear unusual stories and muster
As much enthusiasm as I can —
When I arrive at my desk following
The meditation and the circle I

Hunt for inspiration in the sky and
I'm not trying to be happy but I'm
Waiting for an appropriate word to
Apply to an emerging stream of thought

And nothing so far has brought me greater
Satisfaction than morning clarity.

Where I go and what
I do with myself creates
organization
sets the circumstances and
gratitude is natural.

There are moments of awakening that
Aren't altogether enjoyable in
The winter months of Minnesota and
When walking on the asphalt or concrete

After a drizzling that froze into
An almost invisible layer of
Ice we learn to look for a glint of light
Reflecting off the walkway because a

Second's carelessness leads to a quirky
Jerk to discombobulation to an
Impactful connection with a very
Hard surface after which we're completely

Awake realizing penetrating
Insight into the quality of now.

Because I'm spry I
jerk discombobulate but
sometimes I'm able
to catch myself before the
fall discovering balance.

It's not so remarkable — the stainless
Steel the simple utility — it's a
Common implement every household has
So many of but this morning I see

The spoon is composed of sinuous lines
Complementing my fingers and the bowl
Is formed of circles within circles of
Diminishing size perfect for holding

Granola banana blue berries and
Skim milk and I'm not a chimpanzee and
Didn't invent these things myself or pick
The berries or milk the cow — this morning

I recognize all the gifts of breakfast —
Granola banana berries and milk.

Watching the news on
television while eating
breakfast amounts to
mindlessly munching staring —
someone else does my thinking.

Saturday is not an ordinary
Day for me because we assemble in
A chapel with the dawn to meditate
And sharing the quiet enhances the

Quiet communing peacefully deepens
The peace and as thoughts arise we practice
Immobility and as emotions
Emerge we let them go and each journeys

Uniquely and each delves separately but
There's a commonality to human
Consciousness as we derive energy
From each other and together we learn

That agitation is momentary
And cultivated peace is powerful.

I'm not finished yet
not a master of repose
within this moment
and don't have walk-around poise
but I would like to be so.

Circumstances coordinate outcomes
Not always to my satisfaction as
I encountered the invisible ice
While driving down a sloping street and if

Only I hadn't tried to turn I'd have
Been OK but I did and the car slid
As my frantic gestures with the steering
Wheel were operatic but quite useless

So I smacked into a parked car leaving
Minor damage on both vehicles and
Though it's not catastrophic I'd rather
Have nothing to regret but that's life as

Once in a while I fall through a trap door
Of an uncontrollable circumstance.

The spitting freezing
rain is no excuse said the
insurance agent
as the fact remains I lost
control of the vehicle.

As if playing ping-pong with the cashier
At Wal-Mart I ready my paddle and
Serve with a twist my attitude and she
Counters effectively and while driving

I'm playing with position turn signals
And speed as drivers are maneuvering
Beside me reciprocating hitting
The ball in turn and anticipation

Vigilance aggression indifference or
Courtesy arise and usually
I'm not receptive to community
I'm not aware of personality

As we glide by each other attending
To solitary preoccupations.

Without intention
without consideration
spontaneously
I wallop a wicked serve
carelessly imposing me.

Little Me/Big Me

There is part of me that gets pissed off so
Easily when I have to schlep my son
To work because his car needs repairing
But afterwards I'm ashamed of myself

And I hate my volatility and
I realize I am more courteous
With friends and even with strangers than with
My family — it's so easy to lose

My temper and it's impossible to
Erase an outburst — but yet there is a
Part of me emanating from the flame
Of life — the bare awareness — deeper than

Any transitory emotion that
Is carefully watching and abiding.

I can become
quiet enough
to watch emotion
come and go and
be the watcher.

I wasn't pleased when you failed the driving
Test five times because I was sure we'd done
Enough for success — going from around
The block to merging onto the highway

To parallel parking — you were afraid
Of driving in traffic and I was too
Because I wasn't in control but you
Got comfortable enough and every time

You failed a test my frustration grew as
You just couldn't get over nervousness
So much like me at your age but we kept
Trying and the day you passed I was proud

And now you're leaving home for Alaska
Going a long way from home — just like me.

Leaving for Japan
and Galveston Texas too
I said goodbye twice
To my parents and my home —
It's a necessary test.

A word carries a meaning and a string
Of words make a sentence carrying a
More composed meaning making a point that
May be worth remembering and saying

Hippopotamus makes me wonder why
This pell-mell collection of syllables
Is stuck to that creature because the word
Hippopotamus can't be said primly

Or lackadaisily without losing
Dignity and if you're serious when
You say hippopotamus you have to
Use a neutral inflection and also

The cadence should be a bit quicker than
An ordinary word — so be careful.

Usually I
don't have to enunciate
hippopotamus
or also rhinoceros —
But when I do I'm ready.

It's a dull day nearing winter's ending
As the snow's been melting on the roofs and
A shrunken remnant remains as snow on
The ground is crusty and surviving piles

On the sides of the roads are gritty with
Sand and salt and the afternoon thaw and
The overnight freeze has distorted what
Appeared shapely into desolation —

But the sky is clear the temperature
Is mild and in a clearing between trees
A couple of white cranes fly across with
Their long necks pointing their direction and

The stroking of their wings is synchronized
And then they vanish as the sun rises.

Winter drags and
I lapse into
a languor but
it's possible
to be happy.

Every morning I come to my desk and
Look out a window seeing above the
River valley a far horizon in
The sky and on sunny days there's a clear

Demarcation of the blue sky and a
Wide expanse of farm fields but this morning
It's drizzling and there's only a line
Separating the lighter grey of sky

And the darker grey of earth — on some days
Clarity allows me to see distance
On other days my vision is cloudy
But everyday I'm grateful to have a

Window facing east to watch as the sun
Gathers prominence as the night retreats.

Even the cloudy
mornings are miraculous
once I notice how
an overcast sky softly
glows with penetrating light.

The word processing program is open
My fingers are poised over the keyboard
But I'm mesmerized with the white of the
Screen noticing the cursor is blinking

As if the computer were expressing
Impatience so I look at cobwebs in
The corners of the windowsill — at dust
On top of the books on the shelf — and take

Another swig of coffee putting an
Elbow on the desk putting my chin in
The cup of my hand thinking I should be
Inspired by now and then I see a

Pink horizon with an orange disk with
Yellow light spreading and blue sky above.

The cottonwood the
apple tree and the maple
are dark forms without
texture but as the light spreads
the grainy bark emerges.

Screen Saver Daughter

I've been using the pencil drawing you
Did of yourself to welcome me on the
Monitor every morning and there's not
A sharp dividing line anywhere — there's

Shading creating shapeliness rising
Off the screen presenting your cheeks and chin —
And your eyes are black globes reflecting light
And your long hair is resplendent with light

Because you were already skillful as
A teenager and with the simplest
Tools you captured personality and
More than ten years ago within some hours

You drew yourself — which is natural and
Proper — in your perpetual teenage.

Then I start clicking
with my mouse going to my
usual sites on
the web encountering the
depravity of the world.

The jihadists are bombing and burning
And beheading heretics while the North
Koreans are testing missiles — learning
How to aim — while the Russians have shot down

An airliner — and in America
The FBI has figured out how to
Trigger the microphones in cell phones and
In televisions and they can listen

To anyone — and the NSA is
Managing to keep records of every
Phone call Americans make and they are
Also collecting every text message

Americans send and so there is no
Place to hide while I am doing my Zen.

Zen
clarifies
being
focusing
on now.

It was cold again overnight so I
Wore a warm shirt and put my phone in
A pocket for convenience and I was
Crabby because I had to scrape the ice

Off my windshield my nose was running and
I felt a cold coming on and moving
Was difficult and then my phone started
Ringing and I grumbled — who's calling me

Now and I'm not unzipping my coat to
Get to the phone — and then I realized
Because my ringtone is the singing of
A robin — I was wrong — it wasn't the

Phone but a robin I was hearing on
A chilly morning on the verge of spring.

And with a woozy
head a sloppy nose and moving
with difficulty
I felt a little foolish
and a little happier.

There's a glow inside that's not due to the
Caffeine in my coffee not discouraged
By the damp and gloom of an overcast
Morning in April after a night of

Rain and it's not exhilaration or
Excitement and if I weren't alert I
Wouldn't notice and if I hadn't had
Troubles it wouldn't be noticeable —

Like a lamp in the night I'm cheered on a
Gloomy day because somehow I believe
My being is indestructible and
However many mistakes I've made I

Am a flame glimmering in the darkness
And the darkness is inspired with life.

I see persistence
in the roots in the thickness
in the greening of
the grass again in April
as the sun begins to burn.

There is music before dawn as the birds
Have returned and though the grass is crunchy
With frost underfoot the deep freeze will be
Lifting from the earth precipitously

And already there are eagles skimming
Currents of air and soon there'll be swallows
Cutting the air and when I see bees buzz
In summer I will wear as little as

Possible — Imagine seeing the earth
From the vantage of the moon with God's eyes
As it circles the sun and revolves on
Its axis — wouldn't the dawning light be

So much like a wave ceaselessly cresting
With night receding and blue sky surging?

Acquire perspective
indulge imagination
because it's a gift
to be lost in wonderment
and to ponder why we're here.

It's cloudy along the horizon and
Above there's a single cloud that looks like
The strokes of a brush transforming in the
Wind and then a blur of movement becomes

Sparrows alighting in the cottonwood
The maple and the apple tree and as
They fly and vanish I see on every
Branch of every tree buds are emerging —

I can't stay long because there's work to do
And nobody's paying me to loiter
But I linger long enough to take a
Breath and close my eyes and see my lids are

Red with the light and there is the touch
Of sun on my face and wind in my ears.

There is no other
time but now as the
sky is hiding the
stars and I'm busy —
I can loiter.

Crossing a threshold and absorbing light
There's a connection to be imagined
In a baby seeing swirls of color
And hearing startling and soothing sounds

Experiencing taste distinguishing
The warming power of a smiling face
A comforting voice with an embrace — and
As leaves of the trees emerge and absorb

The light as the roots consume nutrients
From a thawing soil the tree will never
Know it's a tree — but when the gnawing of
Hunger comes the baby discovers how

To manipulate others by crying —
Nurturance arises magically.

Before the things of
the world acquire names there's
no distinguishing
within a baby's thinking
between inside and outside.

A brilliant sky with not a whiff of a
Cloud is a break from the difficulties
Of earning money and the discipline
Required of working with people as

It's resplendent and glorious and it's
Filled with sunlight that happens to be blue
As the sky is showering nourishment
On leaves grass and the sparkling river —

And this is the season the earth responds
With uprising grass and a profusion
Of blossoms and whatever business I
Have within doors can wait for a moment

As I close my eyes and enjoy the sun
And my face is absorbed in a warm glow.

Didn't realize
my daughter's graduation
would take away her
dependence status and make
my taxes rocket sky high.

The impetuous chickadee chicks see
The hummingbird hover at its feeder
And suck the nectar with its long beak and
They want to hover at the feeder suck

The nectar too but their beaks are stubby and
Their wings can't hover so they're bewildered
But soon enough they discover unique
Abilities and flit between the trees

Together and sing their chickadee songs
And they find chickadee feeders and the
Chickadees become the chickadees they're
Supposed to be and if they can do that

You'd suppose it'd be easy for me to
Uncover the person I'm supposed to be.

Do I resemble
an eagle a peacock a
flamingo or a
loon a parrot an ostrich
or just a common sparrow?

Thirty years ago it was pouring down
On the cement steps outside my open
Window and I remember the rain on
Concrete as the epitome of cool

And the steady pattering was welcome
As an oasis that summer night in
Kyoto where it's humid and the heat is
Oppressive and I was always sweating —

I was breathing in the moist air and my
Nose was tingling with the water and
Instead of tossing wanting escape I
Was wrapping myself in a blanket for

Warmth and the melody of the rain was
Like a lullaby on the edge of sleep.

The air was heavy
and I was breathing
coolness and tasting
the spattering — the
pattering was soothing.

It's not usually noticeable
With no bearing on my chores today and
Within the context of our furious
Political warfare it's laughable

But a sunrise with a canopy of
Orange and purple clouds inspires thought —
Every soul who's lived has shared this sight and
I couldn't take a single breath without

Its grace as the sun's presence underlies
Our living and within its rotating
Seasons recur the possibilities
Of fruition and ultimate demise —

It's the utter simplicity of light
That it has the power to foster life.

As the sun burns and
gives the earth the day and night
as the foliage grows
and provides breathable air
I have to make my choices.

The eagle sways and drifts in currents of
Air skimming and unconcerned about the
Direction of the wind as it's hunting
And following the movement of fish in

The water as the buffeting of wind and
The adjusting of wings and tail feathers
Comes as naturally as breathing and
If it chose instantaneously it

Would drop and strike with its talons to crush
And tear with a mighty grip and so death
Happens suddenly in the world and as
A symbol for comprehending eyes the

Eagle is a magnificent image —
Everything I know could instantly end.

There's night and day and
spring summer fall and winter
there's youth and aging
and my preoccupations —
just temporarily so.

I love my eyesight but there came a point
When reading became difficult and my
Eyes today often feel tired — imagine
Unlimited vision three hundred and

Sixty degrees from a point that's also
Unlimited that in a whim could go
Anywhere — and imagine seeing from
Here to whatever edge the expanding

Universe has — and then imagine each
Sensation similarly unbounded
By space and time and the constrictions of
A personality suffering the

Vulnerabilities inherent in
In a body destined to disappear.

I can't
Imagine a
Consciousness
Commensurate with
Unbounded sensation.

A Night Out

To do ecstatic poetry it helps
To be in ecstasy I suppose and
I went to a gathering of Rumi
Enthusiasts and with my friends we heard

Music with repetitive lyrics with
Pulsating rhythm and frequently I
Felt in the singers' vibrato both
Sorrow and joy indistinguishable

And the words of the poetry spoke of
Drums and tambourines of stars and moon — of
Dissolving inside and outside and of
Opening the door to visitations

Of all emotions without favorites
And most of all I heard about the friend.

Dancing one circle
Inside another holding
Hands and rotating
In opposite directions
we greeted ourselves in turn.

Perhaps I've been a little careless in
Raising my kids and perhaps I was too
Self-absorbed to give much thought to molding
Their personalities as I let them

Grow without weeding but — like a bolt of
Lighting — I was hit with a memory
Of the frown my father imposed on me
Because the frown communicated such

Embarrassment and disapproval and
I felt shame — and anger — that he would be
So aggressive — then shame and dependence
Began to percolate with rebellion —

One generation after another
We do perpetuate imperfections.

We muddle through with
dispositions attitudes
personality
imposing on each other
without recognizing how.

As one of billions I don't amount to
Much but as a dad I'm a colossus
To a son and daughter from the moment
When I held them after they were born to

Their graduation from college into
Today I've fretted about their prospects
I've witnessed the procession of friends the
Dissolution of friendships — I've been there

When they became secretive I became
Tiresome and disappointing to them
When they resisted my guidance and deeds
Because I didn't know how to deflect

The silence and just as they're becoming
Confident and productive they're leaving.

There are days in the
year each of us celebrate
that acquire more
significance as we age
and for me it's father's day.

Just wisps of clouds are drifting along and
Could any image be more opposed to
Concentrating on the second hand as
It ticks across the numbers of a watch?

And I may choose either method to mark
The passage of time and whether I look
Up or down depends at the moment on
How much pressure I allow myself to

Feel — the numbers represent the need for
Organization as nothing worthy
Gets done without the efficient use of
Time and yet when I see the clouds I do

Remember in the midst of bustle I
Want to embody a cloud's deportment.

To emulate a
cloud's deportment is perhaps
a bit beyond my
present capacity but
I want less frenzied thinking.

At the ending of a downpour as the
Final drops are pelting to the earth and
The sky is clearing and the heat and the
Humidity are palpable the sun

Is beginning to blaze this morning and
I can see the leaves are sparkling with
Drops of water reflecting the sunlight —
But the rising breeze and turning leaves are

Already dispersing the water — and
Then from everywhere I hear the birds sing
Though I don't see them flying and I can
Only suppose that something about the

Quality of this moment has moved them
To a spontaneous commentary.

Only briefly am
I able to absorb all
of the quality
a moment has and perhaps
the birds are more attentive.

Where did my worn out emotions go — the
Unpredictable anger and the sense
Of separation and distance I felt
From people — I remember how worry

Perpetuated itself and how the
Solitary arguments I engaged
Never resolved and how the long walks while
Fantasizing never went anywhere

And I remember the Buddha who said
That we are what we think and all that we
Are arises with our thoughts and with our
Thoughts we make the world and he said speak or

Act with a pure mind and happiness will
Arise because this is the ancient law.

Poised with a
samurai sword
preparing to
strike — clarity
is wonderful.

With the impetus of clarity I
Let my thinking go like a spaniel in
A field of grass and I'm amazed by the
Rambunctious foolishness I see as if

The earth has enflamed the dog and he can't
Jump high enough or run fast enough and
He's torn between the scent here and the smell
There and he's hunting because he wants a

Rabbit to chase and bite — and today I'm
Savoring my simple-minded canine
Energy in love with the enticements
Of the earth and the possibility

That I could get my teeth in a special
Delicacy I'd shake and not let go.

But even in my
reverie I understand
my energy will
dissipate and I'll become
a disconsolate doggie.

A frog has emerged that is the size of
A thumbnail and sometimes it has smooth skin
And sometimes it becomes spiky and it
Is also a chameleon and so

It's called the Punk Rocker Frog — which I think
Is ridiculous because in hundreds
Of years when people read categories
Of creatures they will grasp what the frog can

Do but they won't understand the name when
The species of miscreants with spiky
Orange hair and a dozen earrings and
Leather jackets and predominately

British accents will be forgotten and
Replaced by other forms of rebellion.

We don't use
chariots pyramids
or mummification
anymore — but will
we fly in wing suits?

Some people are crazy enough to wear
A wing suit and stand poised on the tip of
A Mountain and jump — with fabric outstretched
Between their arms and legs and body — and

They fly inches from the rocky edges
Plunging as the eagles do consuming
Miles of air passing inside and outside
Of alpine shadows falling on the slopes

Below — how divine the venture must seem
Flowing within a spectacle of such
Gigantic proportions — discovering
In a human form capability

For soaring with flaming sensations and
A beating heart — and with serenity?

Perhaps a
flying squirrel was
the inspiration
but where on earth did
the courage come from?

Of the things to notice on a sunny
Day by the river I see the swallows
Flitting along the bank and above the
Water encountering no obstacles

Within a wide expanse of air and each
Is turning acrobatically in a
Hunt for bugs they must be swallowing on
The fly and they seem so tiny above

The broad river in the valley of the
Limestone bluffs and so inconsequential
To me they're just a curiosity
That they do hunt together and they do

Return to the river in the spring and
I may open my eyes and see swallows.

As the swallows flit
along the surface of the
river the eagles
linger in lazy circles
up within the sunny sky.

There's not much utility in keeping
Cats beyond the discouragement of mice
But there is the obligation to care
For them within a home I willingly

Do because I find myself calling them
 "Doggies" as a joke they don't understand
Or I'll string together syllables of
Nonsense with dramatic inflection and

They gaze at me with adoration and
I can't get people to do that so when
George my partner in lassitude who would
Sit upon my legs when I sat who chirped

Like a cheerful bird suddenly died I
Grieved the loss of gentle companionship.

Rescued from bitter
cold that froze the tips of his
ears off our new cat
needs adjusting so we say
Henry Henry and Henry.

I borrowed my Dad's glasses one day and
Looked at the garage and saw a spot of
Dried mud so I walked across the grass to
Touch it and it disintegrated from

The wall and that's how we discovered I
Needed glasses and suddenly I could
See the writing on the chalkboard could learn
How to read and suddenly there was an

Explanation for the difficulty
I had in keeping up and I wasn't
"Special" as the teachers said or stupid
As I thought and a physical burden

Was gone and the discouragement I felt
Could dissipate and I began to try.

My brother would fall
on the floor would bubble at
the mouth would shiver
in epileptic fits — but
he became a wrestler.

The leaves are fluttering the branches are
Undulating the foliage is flowing
As drops are pelting from a grey sky and
I hear the pattering of the rain on

The leaves and the accumulation and
Dissipation of wind through the widow —
This is a topsy-turvy morning and
I'm savoring the enveloping cool —

But yesterday the sun was blazing by
Mid morning and the humidity was
Already oppressive so I kept the
Window shut as the air conditioner

Was performing because the pinnacle
Of summer is often quite atrocious.

I accommodate
mosquitoes and horseflies
with a slap — and I
am suspicious of tall grass
anticipating wood ticks.

A crystal glass is weighty in my hand
With the liquid light of the sun and I
Drink and enjoy the water flow in my
Mouth and throat and inside of me with the

Taste of no taste that tastes like nourishment
Like health without anything extra and
Drinking doesn't have to be something I
Do without noticing just as I make

The slightest effort drawing air in my
Nose and appreciate its expansion
Within my lungs and I can sense a wave
Of clarity throughout my body as

The persisting rhythms of life are like
Wind in the leaves and the waves on the sand.

I know the words
needed to find
direction and
then I savor
needing no words.

A wide horizon across the cornfields —
Or a blue expanse beyond the trees — or
The sky visible between the towers
Of a city are beguiling because

Here's the difference between the touchable
And breathable as I measure distance
With my eyes and spot my proximity
Within a ceaselessly transforming sky

But when the sun goes down the dividing
Lines of the horizon vanish and the
Apparent emptiness of the universe
Emerges and distance is threatening —

Reality is layered and there are
Limits to how much I can understand.

My capacity
for logic for measuring
and for ascribing
individual meaning
doesn't touch infinity.

I threw a stone into a placid lake
And waited for the ripples to emerge
As an image of an open mind and
A stray thought that comes unexpectedly

With consequences rippling into
Emotion into behavior and then
Into the reactions of people as
They respond to me as I have prompted

Everything following the one thought that
Arises in an instant seemingly
From nowhere except that I don't have an
Open mind — I have propensities for

Seeing only what I choose to see as
The whole of reality escapes me.

I sit motionless
becoming the placid lake
watching ripples of
thoughts and emotions disperse
pursuing an open mind.

Being in the middle of a lake in
A rowing boat with the water glassy
I'm poised and anticipating any
Moment a jolt of inspiration and

I'm waiting — it's not as if my eyes aren't
Seeing my ears aren't hearing but my mind
Is absent my attention is withdrawn
And I'm struggling to be open — then

Like lightning an idea comes from the
Sky providing direction and then I'm
Able to ply my oars to arch my
Back in a smooth continuous motion —

Knowledge and technique want direction and
I aspire to be a lightning rod.

Does inspiration
come from personality
experience or
the habits of the mind or
does it come from emptiness?

An actor friend described Henry Fonda's
Method for playing a role as he would
Imagine circumstances bearing on
Character and formulate elements

Of personality clumsily as
He incorporated situations
And calculated responses and with
Practice came transformation allowing

The slightest flicker of emotion to
Emanate from a consciousness altered
From his as Henry discovered how to
Lose himself for the portrayal of a

Person caught in a story presenting
A significance worthy of effort.

How often do I
assume a role purposely
manipulating
companions and performing
genuine sincerity?

Some of us are much better with practice
At fashioning a desirable
Persona and added to the gift of
A delectable appearance it's as

Good as money to promenade into
A room and shower sunshine on people
Who are helpless in admiration and
It's a power of brutish beauty that

Flourishes in Hollywood — but there is
A pinnacle in a career after
Which there's nothing more to gain followed
By descent to obscurity as

Other performers take the stage — and can
An aging actor retire with grace?

Adulation and
satisfaction aren't the same —
I want to learn how
to use my energy and
to find a home within me.

The bustle on the boulevards of New
York City and Jimmy Cagney with
His pistols tommy guns and fedoras
Were captured in film with shades of grey and

Jimmy was exciting and glamorous
Impetuous and manipulating
And he turned the elegant women of
The day with his charm but Jimmy's faded

From memory and his élan's overlaid
By generations of stars — and fashion
Has forgotten his masculinity
His desperation and vitality —

He's vanished like the smell of buttery
Popcorn in demolished movie theaters.

Ginger Rogers and
Fred Astaire vivaciously
flamboyantly so
epitomized their era
with swing-time dance and brass bands.

Presiding amidst the nation's heart of
Glamour and gambling in Las Vegas and
Holding sway between flocks of dancers and
Gilding an appetite for decadence

Modest people couldn't afford was the
Rat Pack of the sixties — Frank Dean Sammy
Peter Joey joking singing charming
Taking American culture for a

Ride — but there came a news description of
Dean Martin at eighty relating his
Solitary lunches and regular
Digestion of ribeyes and whiskey with

A failing memory and glassy eyes —
He might have been anyone at that age.

With so much talent
with such opulent venues
and wide exposure
comes exhilaration but
also a tremendous drop.

Clearing the River

Each detail is rough hewn in the photo
Of 1886 from the boards of
The flat bottom boat to the steam engine
And the brimmed hats and the tough working clothes

Of the several lumber jacks with their beards
And mustaches because there's no use for
Delicacy as the river is clogged
With logs in a tangled pile twenty feet

High and the scrawny men in their resting
Postures seem unequal to the task but
It was their business with steel hooked pikes and
Thick cords of rope to clear the river and

Raft the logs downstream as they must have known
How to take advantage of leverage.

Their faces are blurred
but their chosen postures
do communicate
hints of personality —
irreverence and bravado.

Ben Hur 1887 - 1916

It's a day of celebration drawing a
A good crowd to the river and the dock
For a ride on the steamboat Ben Hur and
Perhaps as a part of the festivities

The photo captures the moment and so
I may see everyone facing me on
The three levels a hundred years ago
And each is distinguishable in the

Differences in age in attitude
In fashion in status revealing in
A relaxed and happy presentation
Engagement and eagerness for the day —

So I gaze with curiosity at
An alluring familiarity.

The postures and the
features of the faces in
the vanished moment
present a wide array of
living personality.

I didn't know her but youthful beauty
Communicates the smile appeals and
The camaraderie with her girl friend
Bespeaks a genuineness and so the

Photo of the murdered girl sobers us
As we share it — this moment of sunny
Possibility has been taken from
Her and her child and this living woman

Is bordered in a photo — the man's been
Caught the cause is known she left him but then
Returned and the result is permanent —
Behind closed doors and between lovers how

Could matters have come to this how could she
Have so misjudged him how could he do it?

The brutality
transpiring secretly
within closed doors and
with demeaning words and then
escalating beyond control.

My ancestors were MacDonalds and were
Highlanders in Scotland and because my
Dad came from Australia apparently
Someone in the linage was transported

From England to Australia — this is the
History of my body — but perhaps
I've been a hunter on the African
Savanna a merchant on the Silk Road

Of Asia a noblesse of France a wretch of
The untouchables of India or
An Eskimo and maybe I've been a
Daughter a mother a grandmother and

A scholar a warrior and a thief —
I don't know the history of my births.

My consciousness is
a sojourner of ages
my body provides
genetics but all I have
is what's possible today.

Suppose there's no death and consciousness
Continues and emerges again in a
Mother's embrace gradually seeing
What's me and mine and what's otherwise and

I display abilities and failings
Native to me setting me apart but
Life is a river going on and on
And I encounter impediments and

I innovate and forget and when I'm
Born with new parents the other gender
In different circumstances when I look
In the mirror could I possibly know

Everything I thought I was and whether
I was famous or unremarkable?

Everything in sight —
consciousness and memory
my propensities
my pivotal qualities —
amounts to a soap bubble.

The sinuous dragon flowing in the
Air with fierce eyes leathery wings talons
Appears wild and unpredictable — it's
The stuff of dreams an image of chaos

And a reminder of the potential
For sudden destruction except something
About it has an aspect of purpose
Intelligence as it represents a

Propulsion of ceaseless transformation
A remixing of the elements as
Whatever exists today is bound to
Pass away and assume a different form —

The earth was once a molten lifeless rock
And even distant stars will disappear.

The spirit of the
dragon swallows everything —
the universe has
summoned and determined that
metamorphosis is fact.

Is all of this necessary or just
A little superfluous for the game
Of flirtation as ordinarily
Aren't subtle gestures and hints sufficient

But there's inspiration in the design
In the mixture of the colors with the
Popping of the incandescent green on
The breast the regal crown and the frilly

Fringy sinuousness of the feathers
Made to be displayed as one flicks open
A Japanese folding fan and who could
Look away from the flouncing ensemble?

There isn't an Italian designer
Capable of creating the peacock.

So fashionable
with such superfluity
of beauty — the most
imaginative artist
couldn't dream up the peacock.

I put a dozen peacock feathers in
A marble urn because I love to gaze
At the lovely quills the charming fringes
The blues greens bronzes and purples and I

Think about the bird — how often do they
Preen what do they look like when scampering
And squabbling do they peck at their food
What kind of noises do they make and then

I imagine beautiful women in
Wedding dresses driving the kids to school
And chopping vegetables or arguing
With their husbands and it's ridiculous —

Wouldn't it be a drag to manage such
Superfluous finery everyday?

The panther moves
inconspicuously
surreptitiously
in the night —
yellow eyes watching.

Going to the gym everyday is a
Habit I'm proud of though it's possible
To become narcissistic about my
Progress as I watch my muscles pumping

Iron in the surrounding mirrors and
I've found an obsessive connection in
Pain and satisfaction and I'm likely
To be possessive of the cardio

Machines as I know which run smoothly that
Causes frustration because an older
Fellow often climbs on before me and
He doesn't go as fast I do but

I have to use another machine and
To practice minimizing my ego.

When done I want
a shower and a certain
shower head because
it sprays robustly and
it is the warmest.

Like a basset hound with droopy skin and
Ears baying so mournfully at the moon
And disturbing my sleep I've tossed about
With worry and during the day the hound

Gets his teeth into a rag and won't let
Go no matter how I pull to free myself
From cogitating over offensive
Words and it's useless to ruminate with

Sad eyes with my hound's head between outstretched
Paws on the floor because wherever my
Thoughts go my paws are sure to follow so
I've learned to throw the dog a bone to let

Myself chew joyfully on projects that
Channel enthusiastic energy.

When I'm searching for
the appropriate words and
images to fit
an emerging line of thought
I don't know my tail's wagging.

Who cares about compassion who wants to
Be the chump because it seemed too often
People would see me strolling on the street
And they'd barrel over me in Mack Trucks

Then I'd ruminate and I'd fantasize
About finding a garbage truck biding
Time patiently watching and suddenly
I'd smoosh them leaving an odor behind

But such cogitation seldom led to
Successful smooshings and unhappily
I became the garbage truck trailing an
Odoriferous load behind me so I'm

Trying to surrender my righteousness
Reactive impulses and self-pity.

I don't have to
squish because I
was squashed —
I would rather be
a Maserati.

My writer's group is questioning "why do
You use a ten-syllable line — isn't
It arbitrary and wouldn't it be
Better to let the words flow freely?" so

I thought about why I do what I do
With an eye for justification so
Maybe I am a bit pretentious but
Isn't my way of perceiving the world

Arbitrary — you and I may see the
Same sun but notice differently — and the
Flowing world can only be captured from
A limited point of view — and besides

There's magic in choosing carefully and
Measuring reveals graininess in words.

I appreciate
my idiosyncrasies
and I enjoy
doing what I do —
being eccentric.

For Paul (a Groupie)

They questioned in my writer's group
"Why do you use a ten syllable line?"
"Isn't it arbitrary and wouldn't it be better
To let the words flow freely?"
So, I thought about why I do what I do
With an eye for justification.

So, Maybe I am a bit pretentious, but isn't
My way of perceiving the world arbitrary —
You and I see the same sun but notice differently —
And the flowing world can only be captured
From a limited point of view.

And besides, there's magic in choosing carefully,
And measuring reveals graininess in words.

I appreciate my idiosyncrasies,
And I enjoy doing what I do —
Being eccentric.

I remember arriving at the bay
Taking my helmet off and sitting on
A bench watching the waves coming in from
The ocean enjoying a sunny day

And I thought by playing the romantic
Role of a foreigner in Japan by
Driving a motorbike across Honshu
I could have an adventure and escape

Loneliness but on the bench I knew it
Wasn't true because an aching hole in
Me reminded me I was far from home
And didn't know what to do with myself —

And decades later I've discovered that
Loneliness pushed me to companionship.

It was easier
to leave America and
arrive in Japan
than to endure time and grow
a home in my head and heart.

Berlitz School of Languages

I remember my fellow teachers and
The time we had between lessons in the
Lounge getting to know each other over
Years in five-minute breaks between bouts of

English lessons and each day our rank on
The teacher's board reflected our precious
Seniority and determined who got
Lucky with fluent students and who would

Be mouthing basic verbs again — but the
Room and window overlooking Kyoto
Was a sanctuary where we could be
Ourselves apart from formality and

In the evening if I had a lesson
Off I would always watch Sumo Digest.

Twenty years later
I remember my fellow
teachers with pleasure
with light-hearted memories
but their faces are fading.

There's a bloom of youth in a perfectly
Proportional body in shining skin
In glossy hair approaching pinnacle
Health and I remember running for joy

In appreciation of blossoming
Life knowing that I could never be more
Youthful than now as the mirror informed
Me but then I compared myself with those

More beautiful and handsome than I was
And I noticed their couplings besides
My loneliness and believed the best of
Life was passing me by because I was

Alone because I hadn't learned how to
Overcome the gap between you and me.

The mirror today
shows wrinkles about my eyes
and less hair than I
prefer but I'm not inclined
to cherish appearances.

Do you spend more time thinking about me
Than I do about you because I could
Be writing poetry and you would be
Happier pulling weeds in your garden

But I'm idly sitting and absently
Gazing out the window accomplishing
Nothing but looking studious in an
Offensive manner to you as I should

Be cleaning the aquarium dusting
Or vacuuming and you're doing your best
Not to kick me while I'm pretending to
Be another Shelly Keats or Shakespeare

But how can I concentrate while you are
The epitome of an annoyance?

Somewhere in the sky
there's an eagle flying in
lazy circles as
he's hunting a rabbit but
I'm far too annoyed to see.

Golden Bumble Bees

My bulbous head is a beehive humming
With thoughts and one by one the bees go forth
Voracious for sugary nectar and
Rumbling bumbling and bobbing in summer

But a single bee doesn't amount to
Much it's cumulative exploration
It's a happenstance discovery of
A juicy flower informing the hive

Where the sweetness is and directing the
Buzzing swarm to the garden that hundreds
Of little bee feet may trod on silky
Petals that a multitude of tiny

Bee straws may altogether burrow in
And with accumulating effort suck.

I may be thoughtful
assuming a studious
expression sporting
a furrowed brow but really
I want my juicy honey.

Love isn't what I supposed it was as
It's a fact buried within a busy
Day — when rushing about immersed in my
Habitual way and encountering

Several interruptions preventing me
From getting things done and feeling pressure
Of not having enough time I got a
Call from you about needing to go to

The hospital again which sometimes you
Do because of your diabetes and
With irritation I left my work for
The emergency room again but when

You stopped breathing and nurses gathered to
Save you I crumbled discovering love.

The experience
was not irretrievable
today but it's a
reminder diabetes
gradually progresses.

As the past lingers the present intrudes
And I mistrust memories as I might
Be misremembering but there was the
Night I listened to you coughing during

A trip during an asthma attack when
You forgot your inhaler and I could
Do nothing — and there was the turning of
Personality from the boisterous

And brilliant child to the secretive and
Doubting teenager that puzzles me as
You remain insular and resistant
To my questions as you're leaving home to

Live in Alaska on your own and I
Wonder whether I could have done better.

Because I see you
differently from everyone
because I have my
memories and emotions
and I want you to do well.

There are raindrops in this piece of paper
And the clouds from which the rain came reside
Now within this white form that was once a
Tree that has become a poem because

Without the drops to nurture the tree the
Expression of the tree the paper and
Poem could not be and the minerals
In the soil also live in the paper

Because without minerals soil has no
Potency and the magic of the sun
Rises off the paper to warm your face
As I communicate to you with words —

The loggers the road makers and the mill
Workers have all labored for this poem.

Metamorphosis
is a fact and the magic
is a mystery
and the mystery is deep
though it happens every day.

The Chinese poets who turned their backs on
Imperial politics who left the
Cities for the mountains and the rivers
Who wrote about mountains generating

The clouds and about the tumultuous
Voices of cataracts resonating
Valleys who wrote about solitary
Wanderings about absorbing the shine

Of the moon in a boat while imbibing
Wine seemed to prefer the twilight and the
Moon to the light of day perhaps because
The dark and stars revealed the pathos of

Being that cannot be evaded so
They faced the bare reality with Zen.

Their penetrating
explorations cannot be
surpassed — their insights
cannot be forgotten but
I prefer the morning sun.

I hope you don't mind taking a piece of
My mind as I endeavor to gather
Bits and pieces of stray thoughts and corral
Them and direct them suitably so that

They cohere in a package deal that's not
Altogether disreputable but
Please consider most of the time my mind
Resembles a Mexican jumping bean

Though I've found it's helpful to think about
Something I love — like peaches — and my thoughts
Become of a piece swirling about peaches
As I imagine rubbing the fuzzy

Peach tasting the juicy peach and then I
Become the peach achieving peach of mind.

Peaches do for me
what nothing else can because
when I focus on
peaches my thinking becomes
peaceful — peachy and peachful.

Sanga

We get along fine just as long as the
Subjects dividing us aren't discussed as
We adore the *dharma* and each of us
Has *Buddha* nature — if only we could

Forget ourselves for a moment — but how
To accomplish the forgetting is the
Mystery we share — and it's marvelous
To sit on the edge of perplexity

Together and persevere as we hunt
For the precise posture or attitude
Which somehow defeats our purpose — after
Earnestly practicing I've arrived at

A point where there's nowhere to turn and
No place to stand to grasp enlightenment.

I can't be elsewhere
if I'm sitting right here so
perhaps I'd better
cherish curiosity
practice receptivity.

In late summer on a quiet morning
As the sun is climbing in a clear sky
There's a sense of accumulated growth
Of a conclusion hanging in the air

Because the sun has spent its fire for the
Year and the days are teetering on the
Edge of cooler afternoons and mellow
Light and after experiencing more

Than sixty summers it's natural
To think of the seasons of a life and
A culmination of effort but now
On a bare branch suspended high in the

Air a sparrow perches and it's bobbing
The delicate limb a moment and goes.

The light on the leaves
of the cottonwood is mild
and as they turn in a
breeze I see brown spots and
ragged edges on the leaves.

My mind is adrift in memories of
Childhood salvaging glimpses of events
Like being with my brother and sister
In the car with my mother driving with

Her admonishing against saying "gee"
Because it means "Jesus" and certainly
"Damn" was out and she couldn't say the words
That were worse that we already knew but

She didn't disapprove of "darn" so much
Though saying nothing was much better and
I felt embarrassed and grateful my friends
Weren't there and I revolted deciding

Not to follow such rules because I would not
Be a wussy when she wasn't around.

Sometimes when my kids
break out in crude language I
feel embarrassed that
we didn't talk about how
words can brutalize people.

I bump into myself when I feel the
Propulsion of the word "must" in my mind
As my back and chest tighten as a pang
In my stomach communicates fear and

I get ready to marshal assertion
And I intend to be determined in
Action because from experience I
Know how shame feels when I didn't even

Try — because I've cringed when I've realized
I'll never know what I could have done — but
I'm grateful through many years to be much
Better at seeing opportunities

At summoning effort and in finding
Satisfaction in doing all I could.

After chasing my
share of elusive rabbits
I'm getting better
at seeing ephemeral
clues pointing a direction.

Of Stillwater

There's the illusion of stability
As one day blends into the next and the
Showers of rain and the transforming sky
From cloudy to clear to cloudy are so

Ordinary they're not worth noticing
And the drama of human behavior
Is much more troublesome and the trees have
Been standing here for a long time and the

Leaves are dispersing the temperature
Declining so gradually but as
Autumn progresses and foliage dissolves
I'm able to see the valley again

And realize the river's been moving
Before America was a nation.

How gradually
and irreversibly the
grinding and wearing
progresses and suddenly
I consider the river.

One after another my thoughts go out
Like waves of light radiating from my
Being as if I were a creator
As if anything enfolded within

My consideration was nothing was
Formless until my consciousness gave it
Being and meaning — just as the rising
Sun reveals the trees the valley and the

River from emptiness — I see details
And proximity — I establish the
Context and definitions — I ascribe
Layers of importance — I discover

How love feels and like a child I hunger
To take possession — and capture my love.

The world arises
in the light of sight in the
flame of consciousness —
I create heaven or hell
depending on my thinking.

Something is always going on in my
Head especially when I'm quiet when
I'm weighing and measuring what you do
And how you do it as there a comes day

After a while when you get the urge to
Rearrange the furniture and get rid
Of stuff and buy a new coffee maker
Even though the old one works — as I watch —

And if I tried I couldn't chatter on
As you do about your co-workers and
About the incidents on the job so
I listen just enough to be ready

To answer the question I know you'll ask
That demonstrates that I've been listening.

I could be thinking
about the doings of the
Hottentots or the
Eskimos but in a snap
I'll make affirmative sounds.

This is an unforgiving bicycle
Seat day after day punishing me as
I rub myself raw with effort — but I
Can direct my imagination to

The beauties in spandex on display on
The elliptical machines and treadmills
Or watch people jabber on T.V. and
Listen to music on headphones as I

Assume the same position on the bike
And do the same motion everyday for
An hour as I measure minutes with songs
And I maintain a loose and speedy pace

And my legs are pumping and my torso
Is flexing — I put my mind in a box.

Pain in the right knee
went away and I didn't
change my routine so
I'm guessing I can ignore
the tightness in my left knee.

Mind is a bowl of potentiality
Open to the sky and the universe
Beyond once I've become aware of its
Quality as I have learned to become

Quiet and to let thought settle down so
As to sharpen my sense perceptions
So that I receive messages coming
In waves of sound or light or by a touch

Taste or smell and most suffering results
From the stories I create by way of
Explanation attending a sense of
Self that is overly precious to

Me — but if I practice quietude of
Thought more of the universe resonates.

With thoughts I compose
explanations for the words
and deeds of people
but honestly I confess
I have scant explanation.

This consciousness I have as I do my
Daily activities is easy to
Underestimate because I get snared
While watching T.V. listening to a

Concerned gentleman asking whether I
Have a plan for retirement because
It would be terrible if my living
Outlasted my supply of money — I

Want to taste the piquancy of this
Everlasting moment even when I'm
Teetering between aggravation and
Grace I want the opportunity to

Balance everything I encounter and
Penetrate as deeply as possible.

I want the bare
awareness
underneath
my many threads
of emotion.

Whether you leave your mark by being an
Impediment or obnoxious to me
I have needed you to set my course by
Because nothing's better than frustration

For motivation and whether I'm right
Or wrong I need to muster effort to
Clarify my intentions — and when I
Come to understand being right or wrong

Is a temporary position I
Assume depending on what others do
I hope to channel my energy in a
Manner minimizing self-centeredness

Because the frictions I encounter could
Be the turnings I need for compassion.

Perhaps I'll claim a
truth worthy of following
or maybe I'll see
how I've been mistaken and
deepen my understanding.

In Australia by way of description
Women who wear their hair cut across their
Foreheads are said to have a cheeky fringe
And I've not heard that men having the same

Arrangement qualify for exactly
The same appellation as it seems that
Men ordinarily aren't so worthy
Of special observation as most of

Us are as appealing as an old pair
Of brown shoes because wouldn't you rather
If given a choice rest your eyes upon
The curvaceous and enticing form of

A woman who knows how to posture than
Look at an old boy without any hair?

Yet many of our
male politicians are quite
hairy — perhaps God
grants dispensation for those
who are virtuous and wise.

I consumed a good part of yesterday
Daydreaming about a romance with a
Person I barely know and though there's no
Regret I feel silly about being

Oblivious and infatuated
So this morning while clarity is in
The air I must acknowledge that life now
Isn't everything I dream about but

So what — don't I know what transpires when
Romance wears off and two people are left
With themselves and stripped of illusions and
Didn't I learn how difficult it is

To manage my fountain of emotions
And two together are a tornado?

Curiosity
infatuation pursuit
come naturally
once we've acquired a taste
for romance — God save us all.

Each morning I sequester myself in
A steel machine and by pressing down with
My foot I can go as fast as I want
And I can go anywhere I want by

Turning a wheel with my hands and there are
Roads to the Pacific or Atlantic
Or I could go to Mexico but I
Tend to stay in Stillwater and mostly

I follow a predictable route and
A daily schedule as if I were a
Mouse in a maze and though I seem as free
As birds are I don't want to go elsewhere

Because wherever I go my habits go
Too and if I leave my friends stay home.

I drive in summer
autumn winter and spring and
every season I'm
noticing something different
that I've never seen before.

That Tree

The photographer returned to an Ash
Tree on the rise of a curvaceous plain
In North Dakota and fixing the tree
Within the grass a wide horizon and

The sky he captured the sight over years
And in spring the grass is green in summer
Yellow in autumn brown and on a day
In winter the grass and the sky are white —

And then the grass and the tree are white but
The sky has turned blue — and through the seasons
Clouds are clustered or dissipated but
One evening a setting sun shone on a

Canopy of clouds producing tinges
Of yellow gold orange red and purple.

From the emptiness
of a horizontal plain
in North Dakota
the colors of the rainbow
are passing through.

Not only the plunge in temperature
And having to scrape a frosting from my
Windshield with the dawn for the first time — but
Also the prominence of red orange

And yellow leaves on the trees I pass — and
The swirls on the streets of the leaves in the
Gusts of the wind — and also the fact that
The sun is lacking the fire of summer —

All these things point to the necessity
Of taking cover and bundling up
For a coming winter again as the
Wheel of the seasons is turning once more —

The trees emulate the flowers and bloom
And then they stand twiggy in the winter.

It's ironic how
the autumn leaves resemble
holiday colors
before dissipating and
I do want to celebrate.

The Stonehenge

When driving along a street and seeing
The morning sun and a crescent moon a
Thought arose of the stone masters who have
Vanished from the earth and all that remains

Are their meticulous monuments as
Evidence of their piercing insight that
They followed the stars and moon they channeled
The rising sun — and the capacity

Of their bodies the ingenuity
Of their mastery is evident in
The cutting of and the assembly of
The gargantuan stones — but no one knows

Much about them and the constellations
Have moved on leaving the stones out of tune.

Perhaps I was a
carver of the faces on
Easter Island and
set them up under the stars
but I'm not remembering.

A rascal put a
snail shell in a
tuba —
rumble has rattle
curlicue in curves.

— *Tekkan*

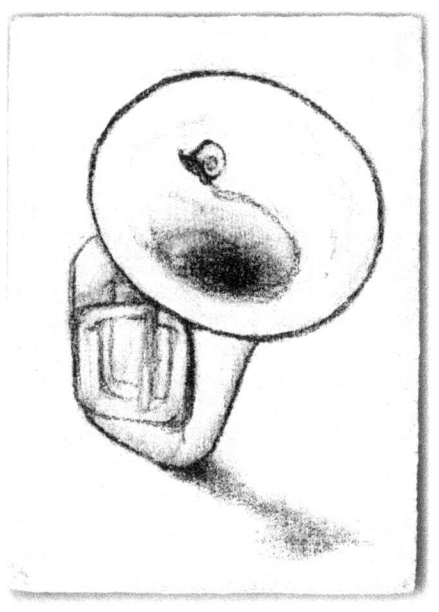

Everyday Mind III

Asphalt Driveway Co.

I was lucky years ago to work on
The crews that put in asphalt driveways in
The summer and we came in tall trucks with
A tractor a roller and a paver

And we were young men exercising our strength
And honing our skills and learning what was
Necessary — like standing on a load
Of asphalt while the soles of our boots burned

And shoveling from the truck down into
A wheelbarrow because that is the
Only way to get the asphalt to an
Odd place — there was no use in wearing

Gloves because they would be worn out very
Fast so our hands developed calluses.

I used a maul
a shovel
and a pickax
and grew a
capacious heart.

Willie's appearance might not impress you
Because he was too thin and tanned almost
Black and the sun is not kind to exposed
Skin — he was silent unpredictable

And volatile — but as the chief on an
Asphalt driveway crew he was a master
Craftsman working from his tractor seat at
Timing the arrivals of the trucks and

The moving of the grunts and at tearing
Out the old driveway and sculpting the ground
With an eye for the drainage of water
And he was good at raking stones into

Place and once the asphalt was flowing he
Knew how to lay an impeccable mat.

Willie was wicked
in his rages over
carelessness or
stupidity or
for no reason.

Grunts

Davey folded the six plastic rings that
Connected a six-pack of pop into
A single ring and with his hands grasping
Behind his neck he tore it apart and

Joey franticly shoveled the stones
In the correct general direction
And Joey drove hastily weaving
Around the traffic with a hot load of

Asphalt and there came a day I had to
Prove myself so I swung a pickax like
John Henry and the next day they let a
Surplus guy go and kept me and with my

Boot I balanced on an empty pop can
And with my fingers tapping crushed the can.

The crew chief mastered
all the necessary skills
and he sits in the
tractor seat and he
determines everything.

A tamper is a steel pole with a square
Ending that is used to put a raised edge
Alongside an asphalt driveway and I
I had a good eye for tamping a straight

Line and the chiefs selected me because
My tamping was a fine finishing touch
And I was happy because I could keep
Working and I had a skill setting me

Apart and I enjoyed riding to jobs
In the back of a tall dump truck wearing
A bandana but not a shirt feeling
Like a pirate and encountering the

Curious expressions of passersby
Because I was a member of the crew.

It is easy to
encourage a young man
and entice him to
work like a raging demon —
give him some belonging.

A roller uses two cylinder wheels
That we filled with water and it's about
Twice as big as a golf cart and I went
Forward by pushing a lever forward

And backward the same way and one day I
Was rolling pressing a just laid driveway
Going right to the edge of a ten foot
Drop enjoying an easy interlude

Between hard labor and I pulled back on
The lever but the roller kept on so
I jumped and down it went boom boom and like
A cat I landed with my heart going

Boom boom and I might have been dozing a
Little beforehand but then I woke up.

Synchronicity —
a mechanical failure
a ten foot drop and
vigorous dexterity
produced a happy ending.

It was a joke we enjoyed — four of the
State government road crew were leaning on
Their shovels as one was shoveling — though
There might have been a little envy too

Because we were like skinny feral cats —
And from the moment we arrived at the
Yard there was ceaseless motion before dawn
And through the heat of summer days until

Returning past the evening twilight and
The only occasional rest was if
There was room for me in the cab to doze
On the way to the next job otherwise

I'd stand in the dumpster part of the truck
With my arms over the sides holding on.

Such a test of pride —
to lift a wheelbarrow
and hurl it up and
over the side into the
dump truck about ten feet high.

A paver connects to a dump truck as
The steel form the asphalt flows into when
The load is raised and it lays the mat and
There's a place for the novice grunts to stand

And stir the asphalt to the corners with
A shovel and because the paver is often
Not as wide as necessary and as
Constancy and speed are needed the

Grunt must fling shovelfuls accurately
And hastily until the job is done —
With the asphalt steaming and under the
Sun blazing if the new guys made it through

The day and if they could return to the
Yard the next morning they could work again.

The labor absorbs
attention so there's no time
beyond shovelfuls
beyond the immediate
calling for utmost effort.

There was a job in the open country
On a hilltop with a glorious view
And we prepared the ground for a lengthy
Driveway on a cool morning tearing out

The old asphalt with the maul shovels and
The tractor and when the earth was smoothed we
Spread the underlying stones with shovels
And rakes and there's an art to seeing the

High and low places and spreading smoothly
And as we were working sporadically
And then attentively we noticed the
Clouds becoming dark anticipating

Rain and it cheered our hearts at the prospect
Of honorably working half the day.

Our hearts jumped with the
prospect of lucky freedom
from a day's labor
as children playing hooky
who are blameless and shameless.

"You are really good at taking shit" said
Steve who was on the way to becoming
A chief and I was puzzled as every
Grunt took abuse from Willie and why should

I take anything personally? I
Could do the work was paying for college
And was Steve complimenting? I don't know —
Summers later near the ending of a

Day some kids were laughing at me because
I could hardly stand — I was five-foot-two
And I looked like a kid — and Carrie our
Chief told them to shut up and they did — and

I was grateful because I was doing
Good work and had earned everyone's respect.

In Oxford England
the university dons
and the students weren't
exchanging profanity —
they didn't know hard labor.

I was nearing the end of my time on
The crews and I had chosen not to drive
The trucks as I saw difficulty that
Might threaten my job so I stayed a grunt

Those summers and they knew I was going
To college but not to Oxford England
The final year and I didn't tell them
Because some might have made it harder for

Me — or not I don't know — but once Willie
Had an easy day sealcoating — which meant
Pushing a broom — and he chose me to go
Because he knew I was leaving and he

Let me sleep in the cab between jobs and
So we had the easiest day ever.

And then Willie said
I would tell my grandchildren
about him and me
about summers of hard work
about this one easy day.

Escape

Upon my arrival at Oxford and
St. Michael's Hall for a year of study
Hearing the pealing bells in the morning
I thought of the guys lining up in the

Yard in the three crews before dawn ready
For a day of hard labor and I was
Grateful for the rich experience of
Putting in driveways paying my own way

Discovering "culture" and mixing with
A more refined sort of people with whom my
Words had to be weighed carefully before
I spoke — and today I'm very grateful

To have known wrenching metamorphosis
And to have tasted whole-hearted effort.

I am grateful
to know the capacity
the precision and
and the talent required
to control a tractor's blade.

John Henry

Another morning sun will sear the air —
Such humidity. The whole body aches.
To rise again to labor hard will tear
Muscles from sinews. The tired body quakes.
Shades don't cool the blazing of the noon sun.
Within a soul a fury wakes to coil
A wrath to hurl the maul to powder tons
Of stone to hide a shame in deadly toil.
Evening glows with the grace of sunset's rose.
At twilight the sweat dries in salty cakes
Across those huge slumped shoulders and he dozes
As he stumbles as he trudges as he aches.
He dreams of mountains cold rivers and lakes —
The earth is so beautiful that he aches.

Shakespeare and Zen

While waiting for a train in Amsterdam
While traveling as an American
And sensing the depth of history and
Culture of Europe while reading Shakespeare's

Sonnets I was filled with admiration
Because I loved the way he weighed the words
Within a line for resonation and
How the meaning flowed and turned and how the

Florid language presented the world with
The lens of Elizabethan England
And so I acquired a direction
But admiration and ability

Are different and I required years
To distill a healthy emulation.

But I must comment
on the crazy rhyming scheme
of Shakespeare's sonnets —
I don't see the need to do
a Houdini trick with words.

Hosshinji — a Zen Temple in Japan

Somewhere Sometime long ago someone did
Discover the pleasing impact of a
Bell and leave it to the Japanese to
Refine a practice to perfect the

Forging to house it by itself at a
Buddhist temple and to swing a pole and
Strike it in the morning at noon and in
The evening and thereby mark the day with

Sound and if you stand nearby your inner
Ears will feel the pressures and the waves of
Reverberating air and for me I'm
Led to joyful solemnity as the

Tone seems to pierce my heart with knowledge as
I recognize such unearthly beauty.

As the bell is a
summons to remember
the wondrous gift of
life so I remember my
intentions and am grateful.

Some of the monks wanted the title priest
And others wanted the perfection of
Wisdom the wisdom arising before
Knowledge and once a practice period

Began the temple was revealed as
It is — an ancient stream — and an air of
Seriousness settled among us and
The slightest harmonious gesture could

Contribute to the merging of effort
With bells rituals and meditation
With a peculiar focus — to study
The moment as it emerges without

Flinching calmly sitting without motion
Allowing whatever there is to come.

Taking the time and
becoming quiet and making
effortless effort
simply paying attention
and letting mind waves ripple.

There were stone steps to the cemetery
And there was a bamboo fence alongside
And I had a spot overlooking the
Temple grounds where I went between sittings

Of meditation and I was taken
By more than just the tile roofs the garden the
Bell tower and smoke from the kitchen
Pipe as I sat on a step pursuing

Just the right posture of mind desiring
The way to extinguish desires and by
The third day maintaining a straight back was
Difficult but by the fifth every ache

Vanished and sitting quietly was a
Joy and each moment an exploration.

Desiring to
extinguish desires is
paradoxical
somehow something has to
disappear and emerge.

When the practice period was done and
The air of seriousness lifted from
The temple before the visitors would
Leave Zen Master Harada raised a staff

And struck the tatami and said if we
Practiced wholeheartedly understanding
Enlightenment is as easy as the
Staff hitting the ground and we couldn't miss

And I remember Master Harada
The presenter of puzzles professing
To be pointing directly at the truth
And some thirty years later I'm still

Enchanted and mystified and pursuing
The posture of mind for liberation.

If impatient be
impatient and if fearful
be fearful he said
In the darkness there is light
In the light there is darkness.

Clouds in Water — a Zen Temple in America

I'm attuned to a joy arising as
I sit quietly with my legs crossed as
I listen as the teacher says thinking
I will live and die is only a way

Of believing I needn't be caught by
And though the idea is not new to
Me that I would feel a joy arising
As I entered a temple again and

I'm welcomed to the sanga again and
I'm immersed again in the presence of
The dharma and and I realize it's
Not about the joy arising as joy

Is transient but it is about the
Joy arising pointing a direction.

Because I've found
the capability
to be at home with
to be harmonized within
to be poised in the moment.

I love a gloomy day with a humid
Overcast sky just on the verge of rain
Because I declare my independence
From circumstances because I know gloom

Is a state of mind I don't have to live
With because I have learned to be quiet
To let thought dissipate and to allow
Emotion to pass without becoming

Disturbed and when I understand beneath
The veneer of thought and beyond the snares
Of circumstances and regardless of
Wounds I know it's possible in the midst

Of gloom to become awake attentive
Savoring the unexplainable peace.

The mind is only
a lens I use to see with —
it's untrustworthy
and easily disrupted
so I practice letting go.

Light and leaf — sun and sky — mind and sky — with
My eyes open I see the natural
Cooperation composing this world
And I wonder at the magic of it

That my skin absorbs the light just as a
Leaf absorbs the light just as the sun fills
The space surrounding the earth with light and
Somehow turns it blue and have you noticed

How we live subject to the natural
Drama of the sky ceaselessly moving
With clouds and rain and wind and light and have
You noticed how the mind ceaselessly moves

From happiness to discouragement to
Confusion and also astonishment?

Too seldom do I see
too infrequently notice
the churning magic
composing combinations
and ceaseless transformation.

Scootering in Kyoto

I bought a motorcycle but didn't
Know how to drive it so I got up at
3:00 a.m. and pushed it to an empty
Parking lot and resolved that I would do

One thousand starts and stops and acquire
The skill of hand pressure releasing the
Clutch while shifting with my foot all the while
Balancing precariously on tip

Toes as the bike was too tall for me and
Through several dark mornings my awkwardness
And terror diminished enough for me
To rumble to a gas station where the

Japanese attendant scrutinized me
Suspiciously — I must have looked nervous.

I was evading
rigorous regulation
as an outsider
as an American who
had more courage than good sense.

Before I got my bearings — before Zen —
I found myself on a motorcycle
One day ascending a winding mountain
Road following a dump truck and nothing

Spoils a ride more so I followed closely
Every turn balanced for the spurt of speed
To pass and I was poised and swerving right
And left leaning on the edge of the tires

Looking for seconds of clear straight road and
Today I don't remember passing or
Any detail of the ride afterwards
Except the frustration and the foolish

Exhilaration — I wasn't thinking
But I was imposing a solution.

Sitting quietly just
dwelling within energy —
I don't have to see
I don't have to think about
anything to be at peace.

On holidays the roads out of town were
Clogged for dozens of kilometers and
The Japanese were stuck motionless in
Their cars while I glided by on a strip

Of the road and whether on holiday
Or taking a day off I sometimes drove
My motorcycle across the island
To the Sea of Japan because I felt

An urge to go and with open roads I
Flew and with traffic I went carefully
But when arriving at the bay and the
Beach I took off my helmet and sat on a

Bench watching the undulating ocean
Pretending to have a point in coming.

I could navigate
I could go fast or slowly
but I didn't know
how to find satisfaction
or what to do with myself.

When a Western guy becomes an English
Teacher in the private schools that offer
Lessons one to one or several to one
It's easy for him to acquire a

Romeo complex because so many
Young Japanese women come hanging on
Every word and it's just like directing
Obedient flowers with syllables

And the women are usually much
More conversant than the salary men
From Mitsubishi who are traveling
To America who mumble and sweat

Who require the utmost attention
Who remind the teacher he is working.

Romeo needs a
modern-day stallion and
a motorcycle
serves wonderfully because
she goes behind holding on.

The sidewalks and alleys of downtown were
Quite littered with parked motorcycles and
Scooters and twice I found a device on
My tire I could only have removed by

Having a talk with the police as they
Wanted a fine occasionally and
They examined my international
Motorcycle license but couldn't know

It wasn't valid (though they held me once
Awhile) so fear and conscience impelled me
To trade the motorbike for a scooter —
Not requiring a motorcycle

License — and I discovered how lithe a
Scooter is and I became enchanted.

There's no shifting or
clutch just a turning of the
wrist and the scooter
zooms away maneuvering
like a swallow in the air.

I drove a motorcycle fast in those
First years across the island over the
Winding mountain roads through villages with
Thatched roofs and swift rivers pushing myself

At top speed in anticipation of
A week of Zen at *Hosshinji* in the
Town of Obama but as years passed
And my daily practice progressed I gave

Up the motor bike for a cub scooter
Designed for delivering newspapers
And it took me a lot longer to get to
The temple but I enjoyed the trip —

It's much better to linger on the edge
Of mysteries I'd like to penetrate.

An excited heart
and surging blood doesn't lead
to enlightenment —
I had to go slower to
cultivate understanding.

A scooter is insubstantial in weight
And size and can turn in a circle quite
Easily and though they aren't designed for
Highway speeds they accelerate quickly

So while sitting upright and turning my
Wrist forward I zoomed off pretending I
Was riding a magic carpet and each
Ride was an adventure dodging between

The dump trucks with paintings of samurai
Warriors with bulging eyes and busses
And taxis that could stop suddenly so
I often felt like a fly flitting by

Elephants careening down the narrow
Streets of Kyoto with my eyes open.

It's Japanese law
riders must wear helmets and
we looked so silly
on the miniscule scooters —
like insects with swollen heads.

Kyoto is densely populated and
I loved my scooter because I could scoot
By the dump trucks the taxis and the cars
As they were clogged on the streets and who wants

To be squeezed like sardines in a bus and
There's no faster way around town and I
Stayed off the congested routes and zipped past
My favorite temple for encouragement

And I liked to see the tile roofs and the
Wooden gates of traditional homes and
The Japanese are best at constructing
Ornamental walls in a pleasing style —

Things are carefully placed in Japan and
Quiet seclusion is harmonious.

Japanese don't mind
Bumping each other on the
Sidewalks as they are
Crowded together but they
Are mindful of boundaries.

As a teacher at Berlitz which charged a
Lot of money for English lessons
I was expected to be at school on
Time or else — so I couldn't be late — but

I had a hard head and consequences
Began to weigh on me only in the
Last minutes and I had a habit of
Leaving in a rush with not enough time

So I used the narrow strip of road by
The curb to bypass congested traffic
And I maneuvered with the urgency
Of a fool who hasn't learned his lesson —

Speeding on a scooter is risky and
Forgetting the time is regrettable.

My necktie flowed with
the wind and my eyes opened
with urgency as
yet again I had to go
as speedy as possible.

It's a youthful thing and requires spry
Ability with a good sense of timing
To drive a scooter in Kyoto as not
Much dignity accrues to bouncing and

Weaving along playing cat and mouse with
Truck and taxi drivers who thought we were
Nuisances while I abominated
Taxis because they stopped capriciously

With their automatic doors popping out
Suddenly — I wasn't deceived by their
White gloves — they assumed proprietary
Rights to the roads and were savages and

Yet I knew every thought qualifies as
Zen practice and harmony is the way.

It's a question of
preparation attitude
poise — leaving early
I didn't have to hurry
so I didn't get flustered.

I was like a water bug gliding on
The surface of a culture different
From America teaching English to
One or a few Japanese students

In small rooms and everyday I rode my
Scooter on the roads serving as the veins
For the body of their society
And there was much we didn't understand

About each other and my scooter was
So insubstantial nothing divided us
Except ways of thinking as contrasting
As night and day but I discovered Zen —

I came to pursue the original
Mystery — the wisdom before knowledge.

Everyday passing
the Kabuki theater
I couldn't grasp its
refined significances
but believe they are worthy.

After a number of years exploring
The various routes and destinations
Kyoto became homely — no matter what
The Japanese thought of me — because I

Became familiar with the bumps and turns
The temples and pachinko parlors and
The bridges over the Kamo River
And in the humidity of summer

Cicadas thrilled and in the winter I
Bundled up and in the rainy season
I wore rubber boots and a poncho and
Everyday I sat on my scooter

Exposed to the elements scooting on
The streets circulating within Kyoto.

I was passing by
impenetrable
mysteries as an
outsider who was learning
to be home in the moment.

I returned from *Hosshinji* after days
Of meditation and was scootering
In Kyoto when I was caught by a fool
In a Mercedes Benz who was blowing

His horn and careening through traffic who
Passed me by and bullied ahead and in
Agitation I followed and when the
Light turned red I caught up by using the

Margin of the street to bypass cars — we
Had words we tangled and I fought rested
Fought — wearing my overlarge helmet — and
He escaped but the police took me and

Questioned the American cowboy and
Somehow they concluded I was harmless.

I already knew
harmony is the way and
anger is poison —
I recognized in a snap
I forgot everything.

So the Zen master in the *dharma* hall
Told the monks about listening to the
Words of his Zen master in the *dharma*
Hall but his time in the monastery

He said amounted to eating rice and
Going to the latrine and his main job
Was managing a slobbering water
Buffalo that went where it wanted and

Did what it wanted and whether he tried
The kindest entreaties or whipped like a
Mad man he couldn't control the beast and
It wandered into the gardens but then

In the midst of wholehearted effort it
Became pacific and obedient.

As the obdurate
buffalo was his ego
he finally saw through —
a transparent companion
a connection everyday.

Japanese make a fetish of cuteness
For children and a TV show featured
The adventures of Thomas the train and
His friends Oliver and Percy who have

Faces on colored engines and my kids
Watched so I scootered in Kyoto looking
In toy shops and department stores for the
Dozens of characters and Trevor the

Tractor was hard to find so I stopped in
Towns while returning from *Hosshinji* and
Found him as the perfect prize after a
Week of meditation and I don't know

Whether I or my children enjoyed the
Trains most but I discovered the toy stores.

The clerks in toy stores
and the monks at the temple
saw me differently
in my rainy poncho gear —
I came for different reasons.

Continents

Angus

As a handsome youth with dark hair he's not
Remarkable but the photo has a
Story — he's just come to America
From Australia and I wonder what

The photo does to those of us who knew
Him as my father appears very much
Like me or my brother at that age and
He's full of youthful open confidence

As we know the story of his life of
His family his ministry the journal
He founded — we know the bitterness the
Courage and the triumphs no one else could

Comprehend and each of us remembers
Differently as each knew him separately.

It's a small circle
of people capable of
comprehending the
photo's reverberating
depth as only we knew him.

Hazel was his sister's name and dad said
She had a hard life as her husband was
A brute character and my dad would gaze
At the photo of her youthful smile and

Her profusion of hair and I can see
A touch of family resemblance as
The enthusiastic innocence and
Openness communicates happiness

But you can't tell by seeing the photo's
Eight decades old and between them was a
Steamer that traversed the Pacific from
Australia to America when such

A trip seemed irrevocable as dad
Left behind his family and homeland.

In youthful photos
of my vanished family
of a faded world —
I can sense optimism
And eager exploration.

His smile and youth are very appealing
As the uniform and the cocked hat could
Indicate anyone going to a
World War and his name is Billy Spargo

And he looks like any teenager does
Though I know on a bombing raid over
Germany he was killed because my dad
Told me — as they were friends in Australia —

And the burst of tears surprises as dad
Said he died because the Allies needed
A show of strength — the smile disintegrates
Distance and time and decades later my

Dad mourned — and as my dad has also died
The story of the photo is passing.

Once the people go
the stories of their photos
go along with them —
we are left with artifacts
but the memories are gone.

I just assumed if I went somewhere else
I would have an adventure so seeing
A map seeing Galveston Island in
Texas on the Gulf of Mexico it

Differed so much from Minnesota so with
My bicycle I got on a bus and
Went south and discovered how to be a
Waiter at a sea-food restaurant and

When riding on the ten-mile seawall I
Flew with the wind but when I turned it was
Hard pedaling all the way and I found
Being alone in a small boarding room

Was very much like being alone in
A dorm room and that I remained lonely.

Being at home is
a process a tempering
of the head and heart —
I don't have a clue until
accepting difficulty.

A song from thirty years ago brought to
Mind the time I wanted much more from life
While I was lonely and useless and lost
So I got on an airplane and went to

Japan thinking I could change myself by
Going someplace else — just as I left for
Santa Barbara and Galveston for a
Season before returning — but this time

Was different — I was sober — my head was
Clear — my emotions were capable of
Adapting — and I was very lucky
To be experiencing teenage angst

While I was only twenty-four-years-old —
And the song encapsulates the spirit.

Briefly I worked at
Jump Academy teaching
children and mothers
English singing dancing and
ignoring inhibitions.

While walking on the street I noticed the
Differences between the shops and office
Buildings and looked for landmarks that I could
Remember because I came yesterday

Knew nothing and was afraid I couldn't
Find the way back to the guesthouse and I
Saw a restaurant that appeared familiar
Got a table and a menu that I

Carefully scrutinized that the waiter
Kindly turned right side up and luckily
They had a glass case displaying plastic
Representations of menu items

To point at but it was a gamble — I
Saw how it looked but how did it taste?

The Japanese
have arms and legs —
they walk like me
went in doors looked out windows —
everything else was strange.

The City

How little emotion the faces of
The passengers on trains show how alone
I am traversing the crowded station
And there's a silence distinguishable

From the quality of sound between us
As if we were each untouchable — how
Indistinguishable are the faces
Contrasting so much with the brightness of

Recognition when I happen upon
A friend in passing — such are the comforts
Of a friend in a city as there's a
Shattering of anonymity as

A smile returns a smile as a friend has
Friends and introductions open the doors.

It's the density
of the population the
possibility
that anyone I could meet
could introduce anything.

I was riding on the train from Kyoto
Where I was staying to Osaka where
I worked and the three hundred yen for the
Ticket was the last of my money as

It took a while to get steady work and
I was going to ask for an advance on
My paycheck from the language school where I'd
Just been hired and as I hadn't money

For the return trip I'd arrived at the
Point of decision I'd been dreading and
The determination was out of my
Control as I was coming to the edge

Of fearful reality preparing
To face any eventuality.

I have gratitude
for experiencing raw
reality as
I've been learning how to
face the unpredictable.

The rules of sumo are simple within
The straw ring the wrestlers face off and
At a signal they rise up from a crouch
And grapple and if one touches any

Part of the body besides his feet on
The sand he loses — and my favorite
Was Mainoumi because he was so
Small going against Konishiki the

Jiggling five hundred pound Samoan
Who didn't move much while Mainoumi
Circled maneuvered manipulated
Leverage as Konishiki was leaning but

Mainoumi disappeared beneath him —
And Konishiki wobbled and toppled.

Sumo's a sport of
strength and weight and technique
of slapping gripping
maneuvering footwork and
of balancing behemoths.

Pioneer Park

A chill touches my cheeks and burns — a car
Passing touches my ears with sound — the sun
Rising touches my eyes with waves of light —
And the city of Stillwater as seen

From a bluff with homes nestled within slopes
With a view of the river valley with
The lamps on the street lit as their timing
Has not caught up with an earlier dawn

Touches my memory with traces of
The boy in me walking downtown to stores
That no longer exist — and I breathe and
The air touches my lungs — and I embrace

And am being embraced by a city
I had left behind but have returned home.

A circle clearly
appears to have an inside
and an outside too
but it's only a thin line
artificially imposed.

So I was in the square in Paris just
Before Notre-Dame Cathedral after
A year of schooling at Oxford having
Scored well with the teachers and being a

Young man with prospects for success who was
Free of responsibilities and yet
I couldn't be happy — now here you are
Accomplished graduated prepared to

Be an engineer a young man with no
Obstacles except that you're unhappy —
Is the world to come so threatening so
Imponderable it's hard to begin

Or is misery merely a habit
You must overcome? You will find a way.

Unfortunately
I'm not able to give you
exact guidance as
in matters of the spirit
we each have our own puzzles.

As if I were trying to sneak a look
At his cards to see what he's doing he
Holds back and won't communicate how he's
Considering his options what he wants

To do what he thinks he's capable of
Becoming — it's time that he makes his way
That he determines a direction and
I know he doesn't have to get it right

There's wide latitude — it's not a lifetime
He's planning just the first few steps and then
He may reconsider readjust and
Change course but how can he know what's best for

Him without testing his abilities
And discovering how the world responds?

Because he's done it
because he's reconnoitered
possibilities
a father may guide his son —
but the son may be stubborn.

Being in a place where a person was
Makes the separation more poignant and
Who am I to complain as didn't I
Get on a bus to Galveston Texas

And take a plane to Osaka Japan
And didn't my parents wave goodbye and
And didn't they watch me depart to an
Uncertain fate thousands of miles gone

And haven't I been wondering when you
Would take a worthy direction but now
I realize emotions can become
Mixed as your courage is inspiring

As you're behaving just as I did but
Part of me I've found wants to keep you near.

How can I complain
of my son's emulation
as Joshua has
decided to go northward
up to Juno Alaska?

Philadelphia

Jocelyn

You were resisting in Pioneer Park
Pouting and refusing to walk on a
Summer afternoon as resolute as
A toddler with a bulging tummy

Could be bereft of her container of
Water that I forgot so I scooped you
Up and we proceeded home — today you're in
Graduating robes at Moore College of

Art and Design in Philadelphia
Which is far from home with a degree that's
A gamble the schooling will be useful
As we have encouraged you to become

As creative as possible because
Your talent deserves opportunity.

The conveyance of
emotional subtlety
comes naturally
in faces you create so
experience carefully.

Philadelphia is a trip as the
Streets are trashy and everywhere grit is
Accumulating and no one has the
Wherewithal to deal with it and I feel

Up against the Philadelphians as
They project boundaries of wariness
Aggression indifference and sometimes
Curiosity and courtesy as

I met a woman who bakes cakes with all
Her heart and she stayed quiet with her guests
While she was watching and she responded
With happiness to words of well-earned praise —

Things may go wrong in Philadelphia
And Philadelphians are quite prepared.

Philadelphians
are sizzling with tension
each impacting each
other unpredictably
so I have to be wary.

City Center Philadelphia

In the sky the glass and steel towers are
Leveraging geometrical beauty
With psychological impact on the
Passersby walking on the streets as I

Imagine meeting at the top discussing
Important decisions amidst the blending
Of shining clouds and blue sky even as the
Multitudes mingle anonymously

Below as cranes are lifting workmen and
Busses taxis and people are flowing —
She's attractive and he's intriguing — and
Corporate shops and ethnic delis are

Interspersed and there's a lot to see and
Everyone comprehends variously.

Exclusivity
and prestige are impressive
but I know enough
to gaze upon surfaces
with curious amusement.

The Rental

The luxury and oversize were not
Choices I made as the ordinary
Vans weren't available so for the same
Price I took the black and silver thing we

Dubbed "The orca" afraid of getting it
Scratched in Philadelphia as the streets
Were clogged the highways congested and the
Navigation system treacherous when

On the way to the airport pressed for time
We found ourselves boxed within an alley
Behind a university waiting
For forty containers of trash to be

Dumped in a garbage truck — as I relished
The unanticipated adventure.

I was piloting
a star ship by the parked cars
decorating streets of
Philadelphia afraid
of a second's misjudgment.

Cottonwood Poems

Within the several days when the leaves of
The cottonwood are finally down and
Most of the daylilies and hostas have
Withered and the pines have shed their twigs when

I rouse myself to stoop and pull and cut
And rake and bend and gather and stuff and
Bag and carry and I move from task to
Task with enthusiasm finally

Once I've overcome the dread beforehand
And on the morning after I'm happy
To have honorably crossed the threshold
Of winter again with the soreness and

The battered fingers and the tidy yard —
I've earned a respite before the snowfall.

Winter approaches
in an overwhelming surge
a massive onslaught
just over the horizon
incontrovertible chill.

If I were a squirrel a cottonwood
Would be my principality would be
My house of many mansions and I would
Scramble over every inch and I would

Grasp the craggy bark and scamper up as
Far as I could go and then I'd clamber
Out precariously along each limb
To find a favorite vantage point but in

Time I'd find my customary byways
I'd establish a civilized routine
Of eating here and washing up there at
The appropriate time of day and I

Would find a very special crook where I
Could curl up to dream my squirrel dreams.

The yammering and
yelping of the frustrated
dogs below would be
hilarious but I'd keep
an eye open for the hawks.

To watch the swaying of the dangling limbs
Of the cottonwood tree in a slight wind
Through a pane of glass streaking with the drops
Of rain and to see beyond the many

Limbs of other trees dispersing their so
Delicate endings in the air with buds
Visible within the grey sky for me
Is to notice the strangeness of this place

That from the ground the trees grow and from the
Horizon the sun rises and we have
Rain today and we're on the cusp of spring
Again and I have the eyes to see the

Changing seasons and the lungs to breathe the
Fresh air and the heart to be receptive.

A giraffe and a
hippopotamus and a
rhinoceros are
especially strange beings —
but so is a cottonwood.

It's a half-grown leaf and one of thousands
On the cottonwood tree and this morning
It's illuminated and flickering
As the sun and a brisk wind has caught it

Just so and all of the long dangling limbs
Of the tree are swaying and so the wind
Is stirring the leaves with a sounding that's
Arising in spring — and as I live in

A neighborhood of trees everywhere there's
The rocking motion and the swelling and
The dissipating sound of the wind in
Trees I haven't heard since autumn and the

Rhythm of the rising and falling wind
Is as soothing and welcome as ever.

The birds have returned
and yesterday I noticed
their singing before
dawn as I had forgotten
their morning celebration.

It would have drained if it were the normal
Accumulation of spring water but
The pooling around the drain persisted
Within the basement and as we behaved

As usual an odoriferousness
Arose signaling something awry so
We called the drainage guys who discovered
I was the responsible owner of

A broke sewage pipe that came across the
Roots of the cottonwood tree — and a ditch
Ten feet deep from the house all the way to
And underneath the street would have to be

Excavated or else I could keep my
Broken pipe and build myself an outhouse.

Before the sewage
pipe broke I didn't know I
could afford to pay
the thirteen thousand dollars
parceled out in monthly checks.

The problem is I'm not evading the
Confines of myself as the chatter in
My mind is trivial habitual
Inconsequential so I gaze at one

Of the cottonwood's dangling limbs high
In the air and notice the absence of
Wind and the half-grown leaves are heart shaped and
They are accompanied by sprays of seeds

Just emerging and behind tendrils of
The tree the sun is burning right through a
Cloud so brightly I close my eyes and my
Lids are red with light and then the cloud is

Gone — all I have to do to clear my head
Is indulge my senses and stop thinking.

Suddenly the sun
goes behind the craggy trunk
and the leaves light up
while the dangling tendrils
and the trunk become darker.

The leaves are dipping up and down in the
Rain pattering on the cottonwood and
The limbs are swaying slightly and the bark
Is darkening with water in craggy

Grooves — Nicholas White decided to take
His life this week — he was mentally ill
Kind and a talented pianist on
An edge who could not be present enough

With his friends — and we gathered and have done
Rituals and are left with questions as
There's music and gentle motion in the
Air in gray brown shades in a milky sky —

It seems the rainy day is like a veil
I want to pull aside to see better.

Could we have
rescued Nicholas White
with better words
with more compassion
and what do we do now?

If the leaves of the cottonwood tree were
Bells there'd be jubilant music this morning
As there's a steady breeze and they're turning
In unison all of them up and down

The long dangling tendrils numbering
Maybe thousands and if you've noticed how
The sunlight sparkles on a river how
The light flickers there is the same flashing

As leaves catch the light momentarily
And they are flickering and swaying in
A gentle wind with the pristine freshness
Of spring and just as I enjoy seeing

The undulating river in sunlight
I am rejoicing with the flowing tree.

The cottonwood
is a mixture of
elements people
considered vital —
earth water fire and wind.

I'm sensitive to dust that causes my
Airways to constrict so it's difficult
To breathe and for twenty years I've dreaded
When the yellow leaves of the cottonwood

Are finally down because on that day
It's my job to dispose of them and I've
Mulched with my mower for twenty darn years
Always bringing on an asthma attack

Having to take in the medicated
Mist of the nebulizer afterwards
But this year I discovered the wondrous
Qualities of a rake and lawn bags for

Preserving equanimity and for
Revealing I'm not too stubborn to learn.

I always believed
in the simplicity of
the mulching mower
but I've discovered a rake
is marvelously simple.

One at a time or in groups in a gust
Of wind the yellow leaves flitter from my
Cottonwood tree — the tallest tree in the
Neighborhood — and I've often thought its girth

And height magnificent even sublime —
And yet every year it dumps a load of
Yellow nuisance on the grass and two years
Ago its roots rearranged my sewage

Pipe that cost thirteen thousand dollars to
Replace — so if a guy could resent a
Tree I have every reason to but I've
Grown accustomed to the ritual at

The end of autumn — of picking up the
Droppings of this imperturbable tree.

It's a natural
monument with a nasty
habit of shedding
twigs and branches I have to
pick up continuously.

Politics

Imagine standing on a battlement
Of a castle in chain mail with a sword
At your side keeping watch through a cold night
While trying to stay warm — recreate the

Training necessary the courtesies
Expected of the network of people
In the levels of hierarchy and
The presence of stone and steel and mud and

Snow and wind and fire and chickens and how
Difficult would it be to heal a wound
How would the joints of the body age and
What would be the spectrum of opinion

About what happens when a person dies
And what encouragements would be useful?

And how differently
would the moon and stars be felt
without a certain
measure of size or distance —
a wonderful mystery.

Imagine the presence of a King in
His fortress while you are surrounded by
His knights with their weapons within arms
Reach realizing He has your life in

Hand to take or preserve according to
His benefit — Imagine being the
King and the necessary precautions
Of instilling fear and fostering love

Of the Kingship so as to govern with
A prospect of success — and imagine
The meaning of the law serving the King
With the purpose of obedience and

Imagine the weight of the fear in the
Moment as His Eminence calculates.

Authority and force
submission or rebellion
with blades or bullets —
someone exercises law
and someone proclaims justice.

On Tuesday morning on television
As the first tower was burning I watched
The second airliner explode into
The second tower and the newscasters

Immediately thought of Osama
Bin Laden just as I was thinking of
Him and so within our American
Consciousness the potentiality

Of an attack from a beautiful blue
Sky was realized in a shock many
Years later we're so reluctant to grasp
Willingly — the heart of our culture is

Vulnerable — in the name of Islam
Some people intend relentless warfare.

Seeing a woman
concealed in a burqa
Westerners receive
a striking lesson —
some people think differently.

As civilized as a sword can make us —
Wasn't it a cultural achievement
To fold the steel in layers and forge it
With a hammer and anvil and hone the

Blade to lethality to inscribe it
With vows of victory and to wield it
Requires a warrior's training to
Surpass the enemy's might in battle

And all to no benefit without a
Supporting ethos infusing courage
In the warrior? As civilized as
We may be in the midst of savagery

Haunting the human animal forcing
A defense of gentle accomplishments.

And there are methods
for instilling compassion
and benevolence
in the midst violence
in the human dilemma.

"Unbeliever" and "heathen" are words used
To separate people into high and
Low regard and it's impossible to
Use the words and not assume a moral

Posture even in opposition to
Their meanings and to say "bigot" about
Someone is often to be a bigot
Oneself as people do divide into

Groups and oppose each other and I see
The categories we create and
How allegiance easily affixes
To a body and I see boundaries

Are enforced mutually by fear and
So is it surprising that we bicker?

Without gentleness
without assimilation
without sympathy
differences are dangerous
bickering is endemic.

Hate

It's used to justify the marshalling
Of power and it's seductive because
It's rooted in fear and with sharp reason
As people do divide against themselves

By history culture ethnicity
And religion and it's as easy to
Hate a group as an individual —
Hatred and war are endemic — and the

Associated politics confusing
As the pursuit of truth and ideals are
Deformed in the process — thus producing
Divisions within a population —

And whatever petty meanness exists
Discovers an empowering excuse.

A mesmerizing
message and a call to arms
in the name of God
is powerful impetus
beyond conciliation.

They live through their wits and expertise and
They know much more than most of us do as
They have years of experience and the
Networks of contacts knowing who has the

Money and what are the intricacies
Of the laws and what are the processes
Necessary to move the direction
Of government — they are politicos

Consummate insiders — who understand
Bureaucracy and taxes and leverage —
And they know how to mount a crisp line of
Attack or defense as the case demands —

And we can't do without them but also
In a free country they can't be trusted.

Intelligence is
necessary for the game
but the nation needs
honest politicos and
genuine public servants.

How human it is to be caught up in
A political discussion and find
Myself becoming agitated and
An advocate for a point of view as

America is sophisticated
And powerful and the nation contains
Energized factions organizing to
Manipulate mass consciousness and so

The news is filled with events that trigger
Emotional responses from people
Who are captured for different reasons by
A point of view and unfortunately

It's much too easy to be passionate
About issues beyond our influence.

It's human to be
caught in a net of power
politics as the
spectrum of opinion is
established and divided.

When the President gives a speech before
Both houses of Congress on the state of
The union in the glorious chamber
Of the capital building his words are

Greeted with standings or sittings and with
Enthusiastic or tepid clapping
Precipitating a partisan slant
Or reflecting the popularity

Of a banality — but mostly it's
Palaver to placate the gullible
And everyone knows it — and it would be
A forgettable exercise except

Washington is a fulcrum and the world
Is moved by people who are devious.

As Washington is
where taxes are divvied and
bureaucrats govern
and influence is traded —
while justice is haphazard.

Opinions vary and disagreements
Proliferate and try to cajole the
Uninformed to profess his ignorance
And try to surpass your righteousness to

See the complexity of politics —
And behind the arguments is the cold
Reality of people grasping for
Themselves and thereby taking sustenance

From the clueless — I see with the lens of
Limited government and liberty
And I advocate for the adoption
Of disinterested ideals and

The cultivation of clarity to
Eviscerate the specious narratives.

Don't be deceived by
rhetoric and illusion
as politicians
are very good at twisting
vulnerable emotions.

I sometimes notice I allow myself
To be determined by the way things ought
To be and I focus on an outcome
And a driving force arises pushing

Me to bring about the way things ought to
Be and whether it's my relationships
Or the management of the business or
The immigration policy of the

Nation I do become quite stubborn as
I can't see another way being good
Enough — and then obstacles arising
Require thought and sometimes it's important

To practice relaxation to expand
My range of vision — or to persevere.

The frustration and
aggravation are questions —
do I need to push
am I seeing correctly
and is it worth the struggle?

I don't know how anyone could be here
Watching the political scene with a
Dog in the fight and not have anger and
Fear arising as it's about who wins

And loses — and the loss is real or seems
So — and as I share with my *sangha* and
Discuss the *dharma* and believe that hate
Does not diminish hate but love does — and

As I cherish the direction and can
Almost penetrate the boundary of the
Ethereal — I am living in the
Realm of passions and of gain and loss and

However much my intellect absorbs —
I don't know how to liberate my heart.

I believe that words
alone are insufficient
that the *dharma* points
the way to liberation —
and liberation happens.

I'm lucky to have found ideals for the
Most humane and liberating form of
Government that are culled from history
Economics experimentation

And *The Federalist Papers* on the
Motives of humanity with a view
Of natural law — but if I encounter
Unscrupulous opposition and if

My reputation is diminished and my
Livelihood is jeopardized I wouldn't
Be surprised — because the advancement of
Ideals is risky — but I'm lucky because

I've also entered the *Buddha* way and
I know how to practice and be quiet.

Judeo-Christian
Greco-Roman ideals
may liberalize
much of society — and
meditation is lovely.

Racism does exist and it's a fear
Of strangers based on appearance and it's
An ancient hatred abiding in the
World but the word "racist" is used as a

Smear of groups of people whose hearts and minds
The politico shouldn't judge — as he
Is attacking masses of strangers he
Doesn't know based on their appearance — and

He is cultivating resentful minds
Among his followers — redirecting
Hatred — perpetuating precisely
The same evil he is accusing his

Targets of because he's doesn't desire
Reconciliation he wants power.

Today's politics
involves manipulating
mass consciousness to
delegitimize targets
depersonalize people.

In a "half-faced camp" a shed with three sides
They lived not much better than bears in a
Cave because that's the best Thomas could do
Hewing a shelter from the woods with an

Ax and saw — they arrived after fourteen
Days in an oxen caravan to a
Fork on the Sangamon River to a
Place without obligations and to a

Site where Nancy his mother would die from
Milk sickness where Abraham learned to do
Sums of arithmetic by writing on
A wooden shovel and shaving it off —

He had a year's schooling but he absorbed
The Bible and Robinson Crusoe.

Weighing his words and
speaking dispassionately
Abraham Lincoln
would present his arguments
sincerely and precisely.

Abraham Lincoln

He was moved with compassion for the slaves
Declared the nation must choose slavery or
Freedom when none wanted to see the truth
He knew the choice could not be evaded —

Thoughtful and grave with a far-away gaze
Burdens settled on him as he became
The master of himself and of many
Hot-tempered men contesting Civil War —

The north fought to preserve union and law —
Not to free slaves — Lincoln understood the
Temper of his people knew not to waste
The slaughter of soldiers so he waited

Until emancipation could succeed —
He was the only one fit for the job.

Sadness troubled him
compassion moved him to lead
strength sustained him through
thousands of battlefield deaths —
may he be honored always.

Blunderbuss

It's ornate on the hill overlooking
The valley just below the historic
Courthouse and the memorial for those
Of the First Minnesota who died at

Gettysburg with its thick layering of
Brown paint on its carriage and with its dense
Coating of black the cannon seems a bit
Unreal — but I'm impressed by its size and

Its design — because there's nothing graceful
About it because it's meant for slaughtering
Soldiers and — perhaps it's the distance in
Time and from a battlefield that creates

A ceremonial vibe — but to me
It represents ruthless brutality.

The bronze statue of
the union soldier with his
bayonet fixed is
advancing — and concealing
the terror he must have felt.

If I don't surrender belligerence
I won't find the balance I need — if I
Don't acknowledge my defiance I won't
Escape my frustrations and self-pity —

Because people and situations are
Like mirrors reflecting back to me the
Attitudes and emotions I carry
And every justification even

Justified reasoning if taken with
Truculence rebounds to punish me — so
How do I function within a world that's
Divided into warring factions when

With good intentions I believe I'm called
To be political and to persist?

I want to be as
articulate confident
and determined as
possible — and I also
want to avoid bitterness.

Myths and Dreams

It came from the ancient Greeks whom we don't
Understand — from a poet's telling of
A warrior's long journey home — and the
Obstacles he defeats with persistence

Resourcefulness trickery — and it seems
A violent phantasmagoria —
When intelligence and brutality
Were admired — and often survival

Was hand to mouth — and so Odysseus
Lulls the Cyclopes into drunkenness and
Puts out its eye with a burning stake and
His companions aren't eaten — and I can

Imagine horror and despondency
Turned to euphoria and victory.

We don't control the
inspiration of dreams of
the visitation
of primal reality —
visceral memory.

Daedalus was a such a magician the
King demanded his allegiance but as
Daedalus was also particular
He would not serve — so he fashioned wings of

Wax and feathers for himself and his son
To flee from Crete — and he advised the youth
Not to fly too near the sun because the
Design was fallible and required

Careful use — but because Icarus was
Young and impetuous he could not be
Reasonable with a gift of divine
Power — so he flew too high and the wax

Melted and the wings disintegrated
As Daedalus watched and could do nothing.

As Icarus plunged
into the sea Daedalus
realized the cost
of divine inspiration —
without due humility.

With satellites compassing the earth and
Ubiquitous video and instant
Communication there's no place beyond
Reach anymore as long as a person's

Properly plugged in to modernity —
As the quicksilver god Hermes has been
Left behind a swift jetliner gasping —
As we view the earth below a layer

Of clouds — and yet Hermes is also
A prankster snickering at security
Protocol and the interminable
Lines necessary at the airport as —

No matter how quick we are we can't leave
Behind our baggage of tomfoolery.

As mysterious
as the trivial squabbles
on Mount Olympus —
human rationality
is incomprehensible.

It's ideal and imagination
Couldn't improve the white gypsum sands of
New Mexico within the dome of an
Empty sky — though it might be better with

No one here because the soundless beauty
Evokes the presence of perfection as
If this were a high Olympian
Plain and people aren't compatible here — as

Trudging in the white sand is difficult —
Marching to a goal exhausting — and each
Step an exertion — but companions are
Encouraging — and the sacred air is pierced

With laughter and the sterile atmosphere
Is overcome with raucous commotion.

Aspirations for
perfection reside within
imagination —
experience is messy —
and laughter divinity.

I looked at the castle of glass in the
Sky and considered how it would be to
See the people below as so many
Minuscule dots — and I imagined how

Daily life would go amidst the clouds and
Light wondering whether I'd settle in
A funk with thunder — and exuberance
With the sun — or would I become enmeshed —

Acting and reacting with the people
I was cloistered with — just as we do on
The ground — but I believe the rituals
And the traditions in the great hall would

Instill a sense of privilege — and a fear
Of losing status — and being sent down.

The impression of
the dream lingered long enough
for me to grasp the
difficulty of letting
go of prestige.

We had a destination and a goal
And I was driving as quickly as I
Dared between the looming towers of the
City at night because the woman the

Friend and I were propelled and excited
As every second was precious and my
Sensations were keen — and then the alarm
Sounded and I woke — and just like a wave

Receding I lost my connection to
The intricate vibrant reality
Of that world — and I grieved for my friends as
Our shared mission was dissolving — because

It was a vital drive interrupted —
And I rose and returned to normalcy.

I love the
the blue sky of
consciousness —
and I don't understand
dreams.

The everyday sky with a few drifting
Clouds is a façade I take comfort in
While the reality is visible
At night — in the black vastness that's lit with

Stars — that's impossible to comprehend —
And however embroiled and compulsive
I may be as I make my choices with
People during the day when I drift off

Into the phantasmagoria of
Dreams I'm in an altered reality —
As I'm leaving the safety of harbor —
As I'm entering the swelling tumbling

Roiling rolling of the mournful ocean —
And I am most passionately alive.

I'm presented with
puzzling scenarios
poignant emotions
unpredictability
forgetfulness when waking.

If I were to play with symbology
I'd create myself as a coin — and on
One side would appear my face with the sun
Representing my doings including

My habits emotions accomplishments
And all my aspirations — but on the
Other side would be the moon and a
Sailing ship amidst a sprinkling of

Stars — as an acknowledgement of spirit —
As I lay asleep sizzling with dreams
Reverberating with experience
Of all the lives I've lived — or perhaps I'd

Be communing and taking guidance from
The animating and invisible.

The days are for my
goals and accomplishments —
but my dreams at night
represent my being — and
mysterious consciousness.

Who crossed the threshold of hunger and fear —
And did it happen haphazardly or
Suddenly as individuals were
Inspired and became leaders of tribes —

Who began the primal impetus of
Craving understanding of creating
Explanations for the sun the moon the
Stars the seasons birth and death — because there

Was an awakened consciousness on the
Earth — as human beings became aware
Of the mystery of our presence — and
We needed purposes worthy of our

Suffering — and though our ignorance has
Diminished aren't we a questing people?

I know about the
millions of supernovas
billions of light years —
but how on earth do I grasp
purposes worthy of life?

Stone Masters

See the ingenious industry in
The transportation cutting and setting
Up of the gargantuan stones and see
The meticulous necessity of

Following the movements of the stars and
Sun for the channeling of the rising
Sun trough single gates — and appreciate
The grace and artistry of the design —

And marvel at their ambition — that a
Neolithic people could comprehend
The vast forces of the universe — and
That with mighty inspiration they would

Expend their precious energy in an
Expression of connection at Stonehenge.

And why did they carve
such monumental faces
on Easter Island
and painfully set them up
under the moon sun and stars?

From precisely this point — from nowhere else —
Does this moment flow to infinity
Beyond limits of imagination
Enfolding every possibility

As I am sitting at my desk looking
Out the window seeing the cottonwood
With just a few surviving yellow leaves
With the blue sky as a background as I'm

Considering what I should do with my
Time this afternoon as there are things that
Need doing and things that can wait but for
Now I'm immersed in the words "the one bright

Jewel" that are used to described this moment
As a moment of surpassing freedom.

This moment is a
culmination of
flowing circumstance
and a point of departure
if I can summon presence.

Indra's Net

Each is radiating the sunshine and
Each is absorbing the resplendence of
The others and to gaze within one is
To see the reflections of all — so the

Blending emanations of the King of
Heaven's net of jewels is a mythical
Explanation of our elemental
Situation from the point of view of

Light and spirit and thought woven in one
Source from which we descend into a life
On earth — I don't know why we struggle so —
It's hard to make sense of so much here and

I can't imagine what life in other
Dimensions would be like — I'm not meant to.

How elemental
to be dazzled by sun —
it's too much
to withstand the blaze
without the shade of trees.

You are a drop of dew on a spider's
Web and I am too as we connect on
Gossamer threads and every person is
A drop sharing connection on the web —

As the sun rises and light penetrates
You and you reflect me and I you and
We reflect everyone and each of us
Contains a reflection of each other —

So much of how I've come to be reflects
So much of how you've come to be reflects
Very much how each of us has come to
Be through the gossamer connections with

People — shining dewdrops in the morning
Sun — I cherish my connection with you.

I don't want to be
and I could never have been
separate alone
within a meaningless void —
I need you for me to grow.

Whether you are an impediment or
Disappointing or even obnoxious
You've been helpful — because the frustration
Of dealing with you is energizing —

And whether I'm righteous or mistaken —
Your opposition is clarifying —
Because sometimes I'm able to admit
Being right or wrong is provisional

And temporary within a flux of
Circumstances — and sometimes I notice
How self-appraisal can resemble a
Fun-house mirror — and I do recognize how

Reckless behavior creates a hall of
Mirrors — and so I need your perspective.

My eyes aren't enough
and I need you to balance
my perspective — as
this world is confusing and
we need to cooperate.

Were it better you be a person who
No longer exists for me within my
Way of thinking and feeling — so I
May go about my business without the

Hindrance of wanting to know where you are
And what you're doing — as was often my
Pattern of yearning — as I could not stop
Thinking about you — but now you seldom

Come to mind and I've dispersed my passions
Into habits free from an unhealthy
Dependence on you to a wide open
Array of friends with whom I've learned to be

As light as a feather — because now I
Feel at home within my head and heart?

No — I could not have
found a home within me if
you hadn't helped me
on the way — so I want to
remember you with kindness.

Heart Sutra

The cardinal in the apple tree is
A splash of crimson surrounded by snow
On the branches the ground the roofs of homes
On a misty day as I'm pondering

The words of the Heart Sutra saying form
Is emptiness and emptiness is form —
Form doesn't differ from emptiness and
Emptiness doesn't differ from form — so

Is the red bird in a white landscape a
Phantom and is my joy a delusion
Is everything and nothing the same thing
Like a bubble that has already burst?

There is a cardinal in an apple
Tree and I do enjoy seeing the bird.

The bodhisattva
Avloketeshvara
says wisdom exists
before knowledge and
she heeds suffering.

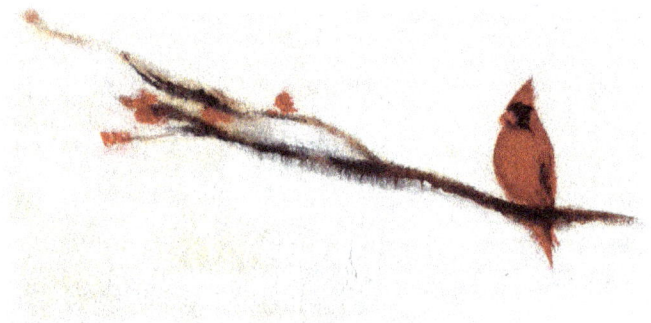

If dissatisfaction is woven in
The fabric of human life and if I
Experience suffering by grasping
For the unobtainable and if there

Is a way out of suffering if I
Follow the Buddha's eight-fold path then how
Can I understand the Heart Sutra that
Says there is no dissatisfaction and

No end of dissatisfaction either
There is no eight-fold path and even the
Buddha never existed because form
Doesn't differ from emptiness then how

Do I escape emptiness and how do
I come to terms with my dissatisfaction?

The Buddha said
an unborn and
undying presence
is woven in
everything.

If my existence arises with thought
If I'm constructing the world with my thought
Then what should I think when appraising the
Heart Sutra that empties the eyes the ears

The nose the tongue the skin and the mind and
How should I behave when the Heart Sutra
Also empties the seen the heard the smelled
The tasted and the objects of my thinking

As if my memory were delusion
As if my habits were ephemera
As if my conscience were an illusion
As if my dreams were nugatory and

This vibrant moment is only a trick?
Then maybe the sutra is just crazy.

From the sky
flakes of snow
are circling and
I'm celebrating
their presence.

A quiet moment is when small me and
Big me are in precarious balance
When I'm not busy cogitating as
The light comes in my eyes as a quiet

Moment is like a lake without ripples
But water undulates eyes see ears hear
And mind thinks and when she enunciates
Words and seizes my attention while I'm

Trying to listen to a news program
As she well knows but doesn't care I get
Pissed as the big me of experience
Seems uncontrollable as the small me

Of passion is grasping for control and
Balance is difficult to recover.

The apple tree
the cottonwood
say we're here
and I respond
you are.

If I were losing
my marbles in
dementia as
I was emptying
would I struggle?

— *Tekkan*

Everyday Mind IV

Watching sails on
Lake Biwa from
Mount Hiei — thoughts go
all the way home to
Stillwater Minnesota.

There are words said over centuries at
Zen temples and they are intended to
Puzzle and ensnare thinking but like a
Jackrabbit solutions are evasive —

A monk waited in line for an hour
And he entered a room with a bell and
Waited until the master finished with
Another monk and the master rang his

Bell so the monk rang the bell before him
And on his way down a long hall he passed
The previous monk and on arriving
He bowed three times and he kneeled before the

Master who asked him "What is the color
— the original — color of your heart?"

Speech is limited
during practice periods
at Zen temples and
silence creates solitude
engendering clarity.

Driving down a hill in Stillwater to
Meet a friend at a coffee shop in a
Hurry because a late frosting in spring
Made me take the time to scrape my windshield

And wanting to be on time and having
Only seconds to spare I noticed that
The rising sun looked like a silver disk
Within a fog that filled the broad valley

And it seemed a cloud had descended to
Occupy all of downtown while the air
At my home on the north hill was crystal
And even though I was rushing I fell

In love with my hometown and it didn't
Matter my friend forgot the appointment.

I lived in Oxford
England and in Kyoto
Japan and other
places but I discovered
where my roots have taken hold.

There are times when I'm habitual and
Not attending carefully but doing
What I do everyday at the same hour
And I need an explosion to awake

But when I'm conversing with a friend I
Get to hear his experience and see
With his vision and in the process of
Sharing I discover the turnings I've

Taken and the growing I've done that by
Myself I could never have recognized
Because the conversation reveals what's
Meaningful and it seems we have a much

Broader perspective together than we
Do separately and life becomes fun.

I am a talking
animal created for
conversation and
if I'm not conversing I'll
probably fall off a bluff.

There are the people who have the power
Who know the law and the traditions who
Operate behind closed doors and there are
Corporations with lobbyists and there

Are bureaucracies making rules and law
Enforcement agencies acquiring
Information and there are journalists
Who write for journalists who despise the

People they should be informing and the
Nation is divided between a small
Number of politicos who have the
Influence and the majority who

Struggle to understand what's true in a
Profusion of deceitful narratives.

Everyday a new
storyline is broadcast to
the nation about
whom we should all hate and
what is the correct thinking.

It was just a twig hanging in the air
Yesterday but a bud is appearing
Today as it's swaying in a bitter
Wind and it's necessary even in

April to bundle up because spring has
A hard time coming in Minnesota
And I can see the tips of the maple
The walnut and cottonwood are budding

Even though the overcast sky is dark
The branches look barren the air is cold
Moist and heavy and a persisting wind
Is lacerating my skin but I see

The grass is stubbornly rooted and thick
On the ground and assertively greening.

Today the birds aren't
singing or perching in trees
they're darting about
because what else can they do
in a bitter April wind?

April is in a single drop on the
Sill of my window and April is in
The nascent buds of the trees that appear
Mostly barren and in the chilly air

And in the overcast sky and in the
Misty horizon — and April is in
The reemerging dampness and in the
Water pooling in my basement again

And every year I know what to expect —
It's time to put away the snow blower
To sharpen the blades and change the oil of
The lawnmower — and I'll look for the day

When the sun nourishes everything but
Today is a mess of saturation.

The crooked little
apple tree is growing a
profusion of limbs
reaching up in the air and
it's my job to remove them.

I won't say it's age as I remember
It happening in my thirties and I
Rely on my memory but sometimes
I would enter a room and realize

I'd forgotten why I came — and I think
It's the result of an active mind that's
Processing too much information and
There's calculation going on and as

My mind is juggling several things at once
Such as the immigration policy
Of the United States and my desire
For toothpaste — naturally my mind would

Drop the ball concerning the paste and that's
OK because my capacity for

It was inspiring
scintillating even and
I was on the verge
of a pronouncement but then
the brilliant point escaped me.

The sun is shining through the tiny leaves
Of the cottonwood making them yellow
With light revealing them for the first time
All the way up the height of the tree and

The leaves are brilliant in the blue of a
Sky without clouds and the intensity
Of the sun that's already well up is
Hard to face without shielding myself with

My hand and I notice a halo of
White surrounding my fingers and I see
All the emerging leaves of the trees are
Shining yellow and I'm puzzled how it

Could be that the air is as chilly as
November as the spring is arriving.

I have to slow down
to cultivate enough of
the necessary
patience before I can see
the flow enveloping life.

I've always looked up to people not in
Admiration but because I'm five-foot
Two-inches tall (not) and to overcome
My stature I became an exercise

Nut running up and down a twelve story
Building thirty times and for the last five
Times I ran up every other step — but
Such deeds didn't make me taller — but now

I'm a youthful almost sixty-year-old
Not sorry I overcompensated
For so long but I've learned everyone has
Something about themselves they regret and

As good as it is to earn self-respect
It's better to become compassionate.

With the advancement
of technology we may
all reach the age of
one-hundred-fifty years —
may we all become raisins!

I would not have gotten where I am now
Without discipline — though I'm not sure that
I'm entirely happy with where I
Am now — because it's not easy to get

Up at 5 a.m. and do the lotus
Posture for forty minutes or in the
Afternoon do cardio exercise
For an hour everyday day and once I

Acquired the discipline its easy
To become much too rigid about my
Routine as if the practice were the point
But the point is liberation and the

Practice is a method and direction —
How would it feel to be liberated?

The ancestors wrote
everyday mind is the way
and liberation
and practice are one so I'm
trying to understand them.

I measure progress by upping the weight
Of the barbells I lift and I do a
Frantic tempo on aerobic machines
Outdoing the young guys and I enjoy

Looking svelte and muscled because without
Exercising at sixty years old I
Could be dilapidated overripe
And depressive and I keep coming to

The gym because I want a sharp mind and
An elevated spirit because I've
Taken far too long to awaken to
The magic and mystery of life and

I want to apply the discipline I've
Won to explore with curiosity.

I could be cranky
and cantankerous
but my body is
a maserati
rumbling and ready.

I've been an exercise nut from the age
Of thirteen with a facility for
Building muscle by lifting weights — but I
Also like to eat so I get chubby

In the middle which I don't like so —
Three times I went on a diet and lost
Fifty pounds eating less and slimming down
Each time assuming a mission watching

Every morsel checking with a mirror
And nothing was more important for a
Year but then my appetite betrayed me —
So I went from lean to pudgy again

But last time I learned about nutrition
And now I'm slimmish by eating smartly.

No matter how much
austerity I impose
I can't keep going
forever so it's better
to think as much as doing.

Usually my name is Barry but
For a joke I'm calling myself Bernard
Because I want to watch my friends say hey
Who is that guy because I want them to

Come to me and ask who are you — and I
Will say I don't know — who do you think I
Am — so together we can find who I
Am because sometimes I don't know and

I want my identity to be clear
Not just an assortment of attributes
And attitudes of relationships and
Memories because it's easy to say

I am something but it's like casting a
Spell and I believe I am what I say.

Do I claim my name
or maybe my history
perhaps my desires —
I do have a direction
but don't know where I'm going.

I live for the optimism that comes
With the morning as the light permeates
My surroundings and I can see how the
Leaves are unfolding today transforming

A barren landscape to fruition and
Just for a moment the quarter-grown leaves
Of the cottonwood are thrilling in a
Brisk wind and the light has turned green into

Yellow and the open sky imparts a
Sense of endless possibility and
I want to be here and I don't have to
Do anything extraordinary for

The moment but watch as a couple of
Birds chase each other and then disappear.

It's not a feeling
that I could do anything
that inspires me
but that I recognize I
don't need much to be happy.

I was groggy when the alarm went off
And Johnnie the cat was letting me know
With is his most insistent yowling coming
From under the door he wanted his food

So I fed him and the other cats changed
Water in three dishes vacuumed around
A litter box cleaned two litter boxes
And then I washed dishes and made coffee

And I made the bed and got dressed I read
My meditation books and finally
I ate my breakfast cereal and was
On the verge of showering when I saw

It was midnight I only slept for two
Hours and the alarm didn't even ring.

Johnnie the feline
interrupted my dreaming
and I'm ready to
go at 12:00 a.m. but
everyone else is sleeping.

Even if I'm driving down the same streets
Every day there's a chance I'll discover
Something I've never seen before if I
Pay attention to the flowing world as

I believe there's always more than I can
Absorb in the moment as my habits
And preoccupations get in the way
And today I saw the willow trees at

The chilly beginning of spring and the
Profusion of drooping limbs are hanging
Limply looking like yellow strings with leaves
Emerging and my imagination

Jumps with the sight of willow leaves flowing
In the resurgence of summer breezes.

I've seen the willows
for almost sixty years —
nothing resembles
the flowing world better than
willow leaves in summer wind.

With each breath comes a tang of water
In my nostrils and everywhere the rain
Is drumming and it isn't drizzling
This is a warm shower and the trees are

Enshrouded in the downpour and the leaves
Are budding again the grass is greening
Again and earthworms are emerging in
The puddles of my driveway again and

This is the day of the threshold of growth
As the earth is absorbing the moisture
And even though the sky seems heavy I
Am happy because it was a grueling

Winter because I was indoors too much
And now the sun will trigger everything

The sky is clearing
a breeze is rising and a
finch is bobbing on
a cottonwood twig and
all the birds are flying.

I assumed the dirt was always filled with
Earthworms and I see them when turning soil
For the garden or during a downpour
When they turn up on the sidewalk or the

Driveway and then they dry and get crispy
Which puzzled me so I spoke to my friend
The ecologist who said they can't breathe
When the ground becomes saturated with

Rain and they're not native but were brought by
Fishermen as bait and they spread eating
Nutrients and depriving the forests
Of sustenance and eventually

They will return the land to grasses and
Put a stop to their voracious feeding.

The worms are out of
control and taking over
like the mafia
infiltrating a village
of innocent citizens.

That the worms will eat until the roots of
Trees disappear and grasslands emerge that
Little worms will determine what the birds
And animals do that earthworms with their

Tiny mouths will mindlessly consume so
Much over passing decades that the earth
Will regenerate — as worm sustenance
Diminishes and their numbers return

To equilibrium — makes me wonder
Apart from what people do what else is
Happening — from what other direction
Will metamorphosis come making the

Future unpredictable because so
Much is going on all at the same time.

I see the world
only as it is
but don't have
a clue where it
is going.

The phones with little speakers that I plug
In my ears — allowing me to listen
To music during the ordeal — and the
TVs positioned about the room — and

The second-story windows — are meant as
Distractions from the monotony and
The revulsion of my exercise at
The gym — and I'm tired as I mount my

Partner the elliptical machine as
I always measure ability and
Effort against time and supposed distance —
And I know exactly what I'm in for —

I will push as much as possible and
Hopefully I'll come again tomorrow.

The yoga pants the
women are wearing while
exercising are
stimulating but they don't
overcome my suffering.

The small room is used for storage now though
The cutting and folding machines are there
With the Ryobi printing press and the
Containers of chemicals and the cans

Of ink enough to print but the press has
Been idle so if I put the rollers
On the pressures between them would be off
And even if adjustments were made and

I inked up the quality compared with
Laser copiers would be hard to match
As the machinery is obsolete
And I miss the rhythm of the running

Press and remember years of effort and
Acquired skills and earned satisfaction.

My dad decided
to print his publication
himself but he's gone
and I am the publisher
and turned to Bayport Printing.

Even the boundaries of my lawn are
Rectangular and every room of my
House is a box and my roof is made of
Triangles and everything about home

Is far from avant-garde but it's plopped on
A globe revolving on its axis and
Rotating around a sun that's just a
Little star among billions of stars and

I don't know what it's all about but I
Feel right at home in my neighborhood in
My city of Stillwater because it's
A quiet and friendly place to watch as

People come and go and the seasons bring
Changes and I'm trying to stay awake.

If I take the time
to absorb the expressions
and words of people
there's a lot to consider
as everyone's a puzzle.

I could make a list of things that went wrong
I could get up in the morning to gripe
About someone and I could nourish a
Grudge from yesterday or ten years ago

But there's no end of that sort of thinking
Once a victim mentality takes root —
But this morning I'm on a mission to
Leverage the clarity that comes after

Meditation to seek inspiration
To cultivate intuition — and with
A settled mind I see the sparkle of
The sunlight among the new grown leaves of
The cottonwood as they're turning in a

Breeze and feel joy in the observation —
Without the peace I wouldn't see visions.

The trick is leaving
my concerns behind for a
moment forgetting
my identity to let
the flowing world enter me.

I am a driving animal who sees
Nature going by who stopped on a road
While mommy and daddy geese with goslings
Decided to cross which made me ponder

Dignity as I recalled the day I
Gazed at a goose and it looked at me and
I wondered what could it think with such a
Pinched little head and then it hissed which was

Discourteous and as the family
Ambled sedately on attending to
Their business unconcerned with impatient
People I granted them admiration —

Without a smidgen of embarrassment
The caravan waddled majestically.

Sometimes a goose is
unflappable and
sometimes a goose is
irascible — who
am I to quibble?

I have my group of sober drunks who I
Meet down the hill from my home five minutes
Away and they give me their laughter and
Ears and over the years in the same room

I've met a parade of broken people
Who just want the hurting to stop — and some
Grow and others go — and it's amusing
How in the beginning we are islands

Of buried treasure and with the practice
Of communication isolation
Vanishes and potentialities
Blossom with expression as I witness

Anger confusion and shame melt away
And confidence and direction emerge.

There's no predicting
how productive energy
will bloom as she may
celebrate motherhood or
become an entrepreneur.

We were given a couch — the kind that's a
Fold-away bed — and wanted it in the
Basement but on the way we came to the
Corners to the stairs and standing it on

End we angled tilted shoved swore and yanked
But the steel frame wasn't flexible and
Lifting was exhausting and balancing
On the stairs was precarious and I

Tore a favorite shirt on a nail I had
Never noticed before and though we were
Hot and frustrated we weren't finished and
I can't say how and doubt whether we could

Do it again but there it is in the
Basement — a reminder of victory.

When the time comes for
the couch to go it won't go
as a couch but in
pieces because I won't go
through the ordeal again.

Each day comes with opportunity and
Firstly I have to feed and brush the cats
As I'm conversing with them because I
Am a talking animal and then I

Attend to water dishes and litter
Boxes and take out the garbage and make
Coffee and while I'm moving my thoughts are
Popping as my mind is waking up and

I enjoy the liveliness of thinking
And I may be looking for solutions
To problems or pondering the meaning
Of someone's words but I'm discovering

What's important for me today and I
Can determine how to use energy.

My thinking creates
direction and impetus
when leaving my home —
I want to be curious
I'd like to be flexible.

There's no substitute for the belonging
And the joy I get from sitting with my
Circle of sober drunks as we exchange
The tricks involved in shifting the habits

Of mind away from taking a drink or
Drug because after one there's no control
Of how much of what happens and of whom
We hurt and we may never get sober

Again — addiction is inescapable
Unless our mentality is transformed
And it takes a drunk to help a drunk and
Together we're strong in isolation

We perish so we focus our lives and
On practicing spiritual jujitsu.

An invisible
and untouchable power
gives me impetus
and addiction vanishes
and we rejoice together.

Arriving at the gym as I do in
The afternoon everyday I opened
My bag to discover two jerseys and
No short pants — so I returned home in a

Fume — and I removed my shoes at the door
So as not to trail in the mud behind
Me and I grabbed my shorts and returned to
The gym but then I realized the shorts

Were nowhere inside the car so I drove
Home again in befuddlement and found
The pants on the kitchen table and it
Seems in the act of retying my shoes

Where I was and what I was doing was
Not important enough to remember.

Sometimes there's a hole
Where common sense should
be so I will try
to remember to do
one thing at one time.

Having a memory is like walking
With a loaded library in my head
And it's possible to know why I so
Often say or do what I do based on

My experience but I don't want the
Compulsion of doing the same things in
Similar circumstances and I think
It's much easier to remember my

Disappointments and injuries and then
My thoughts are punishing — but I want to
Recall the faces and voices of my
Friends and relive those moments when we were

Floating along like clouds and life was fun —
And then my head becomes a treasury.

There is so much
accumulated
experience that is
useful if I have
poise.

Mac Barlass was a wonderful man — he
Was kind cheerful and unselfish and
He was persistently optimistic
And he always came prepared with a joke —

I am in Pioneer Park on a bluff
Overlooking Stillwater watching the
St. Croix River thinking about all the
Tributes at Mac's funeral and thinking

About his reliable smile and his
Words of encouragement seeing the sun
Playing on the surface in ripples of
Light and seeing other places where the

Water is glassy seeing the river
Flowing down the valley to the ocean.

It's easy for me
to be inspired with the
sun and the sky but
night is intimidating —
vastness without oxygen.

Nature is intriguing offering new
Visions everyday as the trees flower
As birds appear and there are coyotes
And foxes about but it takes careful

Attention to see them and people fit
Within the realm of nature too but we
Are subtle and confusing because we
Behave according to unique patterns

Of mentality we establish for
Ourselves and some of us have whirlwinds in
Our heads and others are serene but each
Is busy with thoughts and emotions and

Communication does take attentive
Practice and not everyone's capable.

I aspire to
the poise
of a samurai
awake and
ready.

If he weren't shut in he wouldn't have the
Urge if he weren't bursting with energy
And if the outside weren't so enticing
With so many smells and sounds and if there

Wasn't the magic of an unexplored
World expanding in all directions with
Strange things moving about he wouldn't be
Poised at the door tensed and ready to spring

The moment there's an opening and though
He doesn't like the snow the rain isn't
An impediment so we have to be
Awake when entering or leaving the

House because if we aren't quick enough the
Blur of an escaping cat will be out.

He likes to go to
the basement window and roll
in the dirt and he's
not bothered at all by
the presence of the bees.

In Japan I know it's golden week when
Cherry trees and wisteria bloom and
The air is clear and I remember the
Streamers of carp flowing in the wind as

Japanese celebrate the respite in
May between the penetrating winter
And the oppressive humidity and
They gather in the parks and spread blankets

Under the blossoms of cherries that bloom
Briefly and disperse and memories of
My moments under those trees arise when
I'm driving in Stillwater seeing the

Apple crabapple and cherry trees as
The blossoms are passing by in a week.

Americans don't
appreciate flowering
trees as the bloom of
days vanishes before we
notice but I celebrate.

Of all things they are marks of a moment
Passing in a week in cheery shades of
White pink and red lighting the landscape with
Subtlety that only attentive eyes

May appreciate that make me think of
Candy canes and ice cream and taffy that
Prompts a quiet celebration and that
Returns me to my years in Japan where

They celebrate appropriately the
Blooming trees — and then I see the apple
Crabapple and cherry petals flowing
In the wind and Stillwater returns to

The ordinary hues of the leaves and
The grass and the clouds the sky and the sun.

The dandelions
with yellow blooms
with balls of white puffs
and with deep roots
aren't as likeable.

Sunday

After a glorious afternoon with
An open sky with the warmth finally
Descending everything was bathed in a
Glowing and in the clear air everything

Was visible and the earth was fresh and
Now that the sun is gone the air is just
As clear and the moon shine is brilliant and
Even though they are enveloped in night

The white and pink and red blossoms of the
Flowering trees are prominent for a
Person who enjoys passing visions of
Ordinary miracles and even

Though there's work to do tomorrow I'm here —
Caught again in springy resurrection.

Each leaf is pristine
because the bugs haven't yet
begun nibbling —
everything is visible
because it's not yet humid.

What sort of warrior places kindness
Above assertion generosity
Over belligerence and what are the
Benefits resulting from attending

To the daily passions of life with the
Intention of being harmless doing
Good? I have practiced long enough to know
When I'm angry or frustrated when I

Want something just because I want it or
When I get upset because I'm telling
Myself a story that's probably false
And I understand I have to be poised

Because thoughts and emotions are wayward
Because I'm seeking clarity and peace.

Because I am a
spiritual warrior in
a flowing world and
I'm balancing my troubles
and trying to stay awake.

Every sort of warrior prepares for
Battle and a testing of skills and strength
Against opposition for the purpose
Of conquest but the word "enemy" is

Paradoxical because whom does a
Spiritual warrior confront except
Himself and what is the struggle apart
From the disturbance arising within

His consciousness and if clarity and
Peace are the point a peculiar kind of
Skill and strength is necessary — watching
The arousal of anger and letting

Go without harming anyone because
Anger is only a passing phantom.

Being disturbed and
behaving with excitement
are easy to do
and the universe responds
to erratic emotions.

Anything can happen in the flowing
Universe from a driving accident
From the malicious intention of a
Stranger or from a cough developing

In cancer and the unpredictable
Could happen to me or to one I care
About and there's no defense and it does
No good to be morbid so I practice

Gratitude in simple pleasures minding
My breath coming and going watching a
Woodpecker on the cottonwood seeing
That the leaves are tiny but taking shape —

I see the earth is bursting with life and
I appreciate it's living magic.

I don't have to
wonder how I would feel if
I weren't so afraid
because I'm not afraid and
I believe life preservers.

There's a fire in the sky today and the
Newly grown leaves are attuned to the fire
And the grass is rising up and as I'm
Turning in a circle there's the sparkle

Of the sun everywhere among the leaves
Turning in a breeze and the blue of the
Sky without a cloud appears as a dome
Lit by a disk so bright I can only

See it in glimpses and I imagine
Myself as a leaf buoyant in the wind
Absorbing warm energy but as I
Don't have ability to turn off my

Thinking I can only aspire to
Momentary poise — then go back to work.

There are mornings when
the sun is drenching the earth
making everything
appear fresh as if time stopped
and beauty is eternal.

Once I'm going one motion flows into
Another and I'm able to yank the
Cord as many times as necessary
To start the mower for the first time in

May and I pace behind the motorized
Wheels that set the pace and on the hill I
Have to tilt while walking and I mow as
Much as possible around the rocks that

Border several gardens and this year I'll
Have to trim the lower branches of the
Trees because they've become impediments
And with every step I'm treading over

Familiar ground and I can day dream or
Cogitate but I enjoy the motion.

When trimming the grass
around the rocks bordering
the gardens with the
weedwacker I pretend I'm
a tyrant mowing rebels.

I don't consider there's more computing
Power in the phone I carry in a
Pocket than in the Apollo rockets
That took astronauts to the moon — when I

Routinely talk to people across the
Country while walking along the street or
Get directions by using satellites
Or download wisdom accumulated

Through centuries by connecting with the
Internet — all by using a phone — I
Don't give technology a second thought
And even become frustrated with a

Slow connection as I've grown accustomed
To the magic people have provided.

And it's easy to
forget separate from
the wind in the leaves
and beyond the sky
another star's exploding.

It's not easy to focus my thoughts on
The questions I would ask if I met you
But the chance of our meeting again is
Unlikely because I'm not seeking you —

I want to know why you eagerly shared
So much and what it was about my words
That touched you and kept you responding for
Years as we explored in conversation

But the disregard of breaking off as
You did revealed however much I
Gave it wasn't enough for you and from
The beginning I was wanting more than

You could give so what's there to say beyond
Saying hello I hope you are happy?

I've discovered my
capacity for giving
unselfishly but
I need better discernment
and a little more patience.

I meet my friends in the morning and for
A laugh I'll pretend to be limping with
My left leg and then I'll limp with my right
Just to see if they're paying attention

Or I'll stand behind one of them and lean
One way and then the other and I don't
Need to use words to enjoy myself — I
Don't even know I'm smiling — but when I

Have to take a photo of me and I'm
Manipulating my cell phone trying
To capture the perfect spontaneous
Smile I'm more likely to smirk or even

Grimace because suddenly it's very
Difficult to put on a happy face.

I stretch my lips and
narrow my eyes and
raise my cheeks and
make the final effort and
lift the corners of my mouth.

The grass greened and buds emerged on the trees
During the chilly and rainy days of
April and this year I noticed all the
Limp willows in Stillwater turned yellow

And then there were the mornings without clouds
When the sky and the sun became magic
When nourishment descended from the sky
And the earth was baking in clean warm air

And the cherry apple and crabapple
Trees bloomed again and the grass grew again
And now lilacs tulips and irises
Are blossoming and the leaves are fully

Grown and I'm waiting for a blustery
Day to hear the wind stirring leaves again.

If I'm not awake
I won't even notice the
everyday magic
constantly emerging
consistently evolving.

Eating Out

I enjoyed my strawberry salad with
Grilled chicken and walnuts and French dressing
Because I exercised and was hungry
While you were animated and needed

To tell me about Barbara about
How she told everyone she was giving
You her hours because you were so poor and
Needed help and Barbara was rude and

Barbara de-friended you on Facebook
Again and you're really going to look for
Another job and I don't remember
What else you said but you noticed me as

I was already finished eating and
You were irritated and feeling rushed.

I tried to appear
attentive as I knew you
didn't want advice
and I tried to stay awake
but I wasn't successful.

When I look broadly at the world I see
Wicked people appear to prosper and
Hurricanes blow indiscriminately
And it's easy to believe there is no

Basis for optimism and yet I
Have created a foundation for my
Life by waking early and feeding the
Cats and then I meditate drawing strength

From within and without and then I go
About my business with clarity and
Inspiration comes — like snatching a bird
In flight with my eyes — and I know there is

A freedom of choice with consequences
And then a possibility for growth.

I touch and
Manipulate
Everything
With my mind
And everything responds.

I sit quietly letting thoughts come and
Letting them go and as I'm practicing
I understand there's no control of a
Thought arising but I don't have to take

Ownership and the trick is learning to
Release disturbance and to awaken
Poise and patience and I've become aware
That the earth communicates with me and

When I see the new-grown leaves tossing in
The wind and I hear the sighing of the
Wind passing through the leaves I realize
The ever-present trees from my childhood

Have always been whispering messages
Of consolation and of contentment.

My mind tells me to
manipulate people and
make things happen but
the trees are whispering don't
worry everything's OK.

Meditating Together

The rain sounded on the tin roof of the
Cottage and we were sitting quietly —
Each of us absorbed in our separate
Realities in the warmth of the room —

And I listened to the pattering of
Rain and to the undulations of a
Woman and a flute harmonizing and
I could not distinguish any words but

The music summoned in me a hunger
For a love I couldn't identify
A love not tied to appearances and
Not dependant on circumstances but

A love establishing a lifetime of
Peace — I hungered for original love.

I was yearning for
a womanly form
of softness and warmth —
no distinguishable words

While walking near the Apple River in
A steady rain I saw a fishing boat
Filled with dirt and implements once drawn by
Horses — a boxy combine and a plow

With rotting wooden handles — and I thought
About the stamina it took to turn
Soil with a small blade and I saw
The rooted wilderness in riotous

Growth and my feet were soaked from treading the
Sodden ground and I realized that the
Countryside doesn't ask anything of
Passersby but the farmer here had to

Apply the uttermost of himself and
Today his tools are rusting in the grass.

A single raindrop
would leave ripples in water
for a moment but
in a downpour the drops
are vanishing without trace.

Rain drumming on a tin roof provides a
Soothing rhythm for our day together
As we've rented the cottage for this day
As we've planned our gathering beforehand

But we couldn't control the weather and
Even though the pattering above makes
Us speak up and lean in to be heard I
Love the sound of rain on a roof because

It allows me to feel sheltered — and we
Ventured out with umbrellas to take part
In a soaking afternoon to enjoy
The revival of spring together and

Here I am with sodden socks and bare feet
Thoroughly contented among my friends.

Swallows flitting and
geese and goslings paddling
about the river
aren't discomforted by rain —
but they don't have my cold feet.

Routine sustains me as I follow my
Feet entering my car and returning
To where I was yesterday and taking
My place in the circle of sober drunks —

There's a way out of alcoholism
But not every drunk can follow the way
Because it demands turning inside out
Attitudes emotions and impulses —

I'm one of the lucky drunks because I
Prefer talking honestly about what's
Going on today to having secrets
Because communication is healthy

And isolation leads to resentment —
I'm not that much different from anyone.

Usually I'm
listening to another
drunk propounding a
nonsensical story that
I perfectly understand.

It's Memorial Day honoring the
Sacrifice of generations and I'm
Reminded warfare is continuing
While in Stillwater we relax on a

Radiant day while I'm watching the clouds
Drift while I see a formation of geese
And hear them honking and I wonder where
They are going and why together and

How do they choose a leader and does he
Decide direction and when they pass I see
How rapidly the clouds are moving and
Everywhere the earth is resplendent with

Spring while there's much I don't understand as
Today is the epitome of peace.

If I had suffered
trauma and
carried memories
could I be here
peacefully?

A white disk with a tinge of yellow is
Ascending in an empty sky and my
Skin is absorbing the heat and my head
Is feeling dazed with the force of the sun

And the trees that I watched in winter that
Stood in beseeching postures with barren
Branches uplifted in frigid air to
An overcast sky that were images

Of hardship and supplication are now
In foliage and every leaf is tasting
The sunlight and the sky is blue and the
Leaves are green and the splendor of summer

Has come round again bringing fruition
And who could stand by without rejoicing?

The frosting is gone
the earth is digesting rain
the sun is stirring
growth and the roots are drinking
minerals and nutrients.

Seeds of the cottonwood are opening
Floating and disclosing the quality
Of air as puffs are descending slowly
And outwardly from the tree and a puff

Is caught in a breeze and goes for a ride
On the impetus of a summer wind
And I wonder whether it's the light or
The temperature that triggers the tree

Maybe the culmination of moisture
In the soil plays a part in prompting the
Releasing of the seeds as I'm aware
Of the layering on of the years as

I watch a drifting and flowing puff as
It discloses the quality of time.

Everyday
everywhere
everything
is flowing
in a breeze.

In the Florida everglades pythons
And alligators lurk in the grass and
In the north bears amble in the forest
And they gallop and they scamper up trees

But if I were escaping I'd run down
A slope because their front legs are stubby
And they'd stumble downhill and if only
The earth were a mountain I'd be OK

But I deplore the wood ticks that sneak in
The grass drop on skin and burrow in with
Sharp little legs and pincers to suck blood
And transmit lime disease so the earth does

Not resemble paradise and even
The minutest parasite is nasty.

They are stems and leaves
with thorns for most of the year —
only in spring with
a showering of the sun
are roses ethereal.

A slight stirring of wind is enough for
Leafy shimmering and I can see June
In the yellow reflection on each of
The cottonwood leaves and I can see the

White disk with yellow radiance as the
Sun is setting as heat is lingering
In the air and to the east the sky is
Pale and the leaves of trees are a dark mass —

I am a remembering creature with
Images of the snow in the wind in
My head with knowledge of the summer and
Winter solstice incessantly coming —

I'm knowledgeable enough to use words
And to appreciate a summer sun.

The sun swelters in
July and early August
and the grass burns and
turns brown and humidity
makes my breathing difficult.

Craig

You are a remembering animal
Telling me about the moon and you and
The black wolf considering each other
Telling me about the fifty deer you

Shot as the climb is demanding as we're
Treading a plowed field traversing woods
The forgotten barbwire and the brambles
Telling me about the albino fawn

You saw and as we reach the pinnacle
Of the ridge with a view of forty miles
You see a kneeling deer three hundred yards
Away that was invisible to me

Because I have eyes used to streets homes and
Parks and you gave yourself to the country.

You talk about the
verge of grass between the plowed
fields that keeps the soil
from eroding downhill as
the deer enters the woods.

When I was thirteen my dad led me out
Of the house by the front door and said if
You don't work for me you'll ruin your life
And I thought there's no way that's happening

And I was angry at the presumption
Of the right to determine my life and
I resented the intrusion he made
In my mind though at the time I couldn't

Put my thoughts into words and I didn't
Know the tradition of the eldest son
Taking over the family business that
Propelled him as I was caught in a net

That however much I resisted he
Established the arena of conflict.

Only because he
was a publisher and I
was able with words
did I consent to become
his printer and editor.

I decided not to be my dad and
Would not repeat the drama he imposed
And I didn't want to determine the
Personalities of my kids but watched

Over them as parent's do so when a
Dentist told me Joshua as was eating
Sugary gummy bears I was shocked so
I started saying "Joshua brush your

Teeth" and through elementary junior
High and high school I said "Joshua brush
Your teeth" and he appeared compliant but
He wasn't brushing and a crescendo

Of cavities resulted while he was
In college and I was given the bill.

My dad was a
bunker buster bomb
penetrating deep
reaching the foundation
blasting permanently.

The responsibility of forming
A persona is inescapable
As we aren't solitary animals
And we depend on each other for the

Roles we play the status we bestow the
Love we give and receive and everyone
Hungers for esteem and affection and
Everyone measures themselves by sizing

Up other people and appearance and
Ability and elasticity
Determine how I show up in a group
And what I think about myself and it's

A puzzle each of us has — what are the
Tricks that will get me what I think I need?

Putting the best foot
forward comes naturally
from the earliest
years and I don't think about
forming personality.

My body and abilities are gifts
And I've made use of curiosity
And honed a facility with words to
Probe experience with intuition

But sometimes I feel separated and
Misunderstood and I create stories
And hypnotize myself with self-pity
As I portray myself as a victim

And sometimes I see sunlight reflected
In cottonwood leaves and listen to a
Friend talk about loving a woman and
Hear how a sober drunk encourages

Himself and I remember I'm happy
When I stop demanding just what I want.

I am flesh and blood
and my thinking produces
visceral moods
so I have to be patient
and attentive and gentle.

The power went out in the night and the
Alarm didn't ring but my body has
A timer telling me to get going
So I went through the morning routine in

The dark feeding and watering the cats
Cleaning the cat box in the basement by
Using the dawning light through a window
And shaving in the dark and checking my

Success with my fingers tips and I thought
About the refrigerator and I
Considered how soon the food would spoil and
I was grateful my cell phone was charged but

Without electricity I couldn't
Have what I need — I couldn't make coffee.

Did the demented
North Koreans explode a
missile covering
the entire Midwest with an
electromagnetic pulse?

Our destination is Baraboo in
Wisconsin and they in Chicago and
We in Stillwater Minnesota leave
Early in the morning to meet half way

Between at the Log Cabin restaurant
As we've done for years and we talk on the
Highway as rolling hills farms and big rigs
Go by and we talk when we arrive for

Lunch in small town America because
We share a cultural political
Point of view and we bring to the table
Our differing experience and our

Various livelihoods and together
The conversation is exploration.

Conversing about
political issues is
an American
tradition worth pursuing —
we believe in liberty.

The everyday lying that goes on in
Politics that serves to define villains
To be hated and the righteous who are
Lionized is nauseating to watch

Because I know that the narratives are
Aimed at hypnotizing the masses who
Don't understand the intricacies of
Policy who vote because they're afraid

And angry and the perpetrators in
In the bureaucracies in Congress and
In the press work together to present
Their self-serving version of the truth with

Supercilious airs and whoever
Opposes them is accused of hate speech.

Occasionally
one of the ruling class will
tumble from grace and
with spontaneous words they
expose self-pity and rage.

Reading the newspaper seems old fashioned
Since the Internet speeds the news in the
Air instantly to a laptop or a
Phone feeding an appetite for breaking

News or the latest snarky opinion
And there are so many commentators
With so many competing interests
It's hard to separate the truth from lies

And there are so many people taking
Advantage of the trillions of dollars
Floating around the economy and
Working for it seems old fashioned when it's

Easier to leverage power and trade
Influence within established circles.

News is purposeful
to foster paranoia
to infuriate
to incite tribal instincts
and to protect the powerful.

The morning is for meditation and
Poetry and I leverage clarity
To explore the flowing world arising
And dissipating in sunlight in wind

In trees in budding and undulating
Leaves where I don't have to make judgments and
By the mid-morning I'm striving to make
A living by publishing a journal

Of political opinion my dad
Started fifty years ago and by noon
I'm consumed with personality in
The realm of fighting devils where people

Lose balance while seeking dominance and
Power and all I see is bitterness.

This morning of the
summer solstice the sun is
illuminating
a flowing mountain range of
clouds and nothing else matters.

There are months when thinking about money
Isn't consuming because I send the
Fundraising letters and the money comes
In and the cash flow is seasonal so

I know when the account will be drained and
The publication dad founded fifty
Years ago has weathered the ups and downs
By building a base of subscribers who

Are loyal because they appreciate
The classical liberalism we
Promote that advances liberty that
Opposes the bureaucratic state but

During the days when money dissipates
It feels like a python is squeezing me.

I leverage
morning clarity
for inspiration
playing with words and
hunting the possible.

In Middle America with about
A thousand subscribers I edit a
Journal of ideals and my writers live
Across the nation and I have little

Influence on politics and know a few
Politicians but I understand how
Systems function how wealth is created
And squandered and I've become familiar

Enough with history to believe no
Matter how much prosperity we have
Civilization is precarious
Because the people who exercise the

Power of government usually
Are people who enjoy using power.

Dissimulation
intimidation
manipulation
are useful arts of
successful power.

The most important job I have is in
Keeping my spirit up as I could be
Making a better living doing a
Dozen other things than publishing a

Journal of opinion especially
When the ideals are misunderstood but
The effort resembles a mission and
I believe it's good work — but when money

Is at lowest ebb pressure builds and I
Recognize I'm in the same boat as the
Countless owners of small businesses in
America and if they can summon the

Necessary courage to persevere
Than I can find the guts to continue.

I meditate in
the morning to leverage the
clarity to put
my words together and to
keep my spirit soaring.

For the publication to succeed I
Want to offer a view of events that's
Inspiring and my writers provide me
With history showing magnanimous

Personalities and they school me with
Economics demonstrating how the
Discipline of choice ennobles people
And it's child's play for me to assemble

An issue addressing today's problems
With yesterday's or last millennium's
Solutions and we don't have to engage
In vitriol and accusation so

Typical of the twitterverse because
Our readers crave healthy encouragement.

The opposition
manipulates the envy
and ignorance of
people and their solutions
have failed again and again.

We talked before dawn on the phone you
In your bed and I in mine separate
But communing almost every morning
For more than two years and I waited for

Five a.m. lying awake for when I could
Hear your voice again telling me about
Every little thing and I was inflamed
And excited as never before at

The age of fifty-nine as I explored
What passion was as I discovered how
To express thoughts and emotions that I
Didn't know were buried in me and we

Never ran out of things to say until
You got yourself a real relationship.

I was addicted
to a woman I couldn't
possess and I wonder
is the excitement worth
the ragged end of passion?

The fear was in my stomach and back on
Tuesday when I was thinking about the
Future without any surety of
What or who will be with me — and ragged

Fear was the acid hollowness in my
Gut — was the tension in my back — but like
Any emotion does the fear dissolved
And today I'm drawing encouragement

From the gentleness of the breeze in the
Leaves and I'm wondering if love is like
The wind the water and the light as love
Is transparent by itself and only

In relation to something and someone
Else does love emerge to soothe my spirit.

I'm imagining
everywhere I go today
original love —
a mother's love — is with me
and I'm really not alone.

The wood flooring of the Zen temple was
Old and the boards were worn by the feet of
Generations and they creaked underfoot
As we walked mindfully as the footing

Was unsteady and sitting in the hall
Listening to people walking engaged
Me as we practiced quiet watchfulness
Because the stepping was impressive and

As I'm practicing quiet watchfulness
Today I realize how much my mind
Resembles the flooring of the temple
Worn with experience into patterns

As I'm sitting in the hall of my mind
Listening I enjoy the morning sun.

Thought is only thought
and often repetitive —
I want to sit in
a sacred place absorbing
magical emanations.

I thought Zen was in the lotus posture
While sitting all day — for day after day —
At the temple like a breathing statue
With legs crossed and feet on thighs and back straight

I told myself that relaxing would be
A failure and I endured needlessly
Because I hadn't discovered my Zen
Compass — there is no need to be extra

Ordinary that the only reason
For the posture is to position the
Mind to be alert and open like a bowl
As thinking and emotion come and go

Without me interfering so I may
Awake to vagaries of mind flowing.

The world appears
according to the
quality of my
perceptions and
actions.

Everyone is free to think whatever
They want about the end of life but it's
Difficult to see with fresh eyes because
Dogma limits the imagination

But the simple wording of the Dalai Lama —
No beginning no ending — resonates
With me because he's not asserting his
Certainty but embracing mystery

As the faces and voices of people
Who disappeared are lingering in my
Memory Dalai enables me to
Relax by suggesting I only have

To live in this moment this place because
Everything and everyone begins here.

People I don't see
anymore are with me and
we are becoming
a caravan traveling
under a resplendent sky.

I wonder whether I wore silk robes and
Used an ivory comb and selected the
Most beautiful woman and I wonder
Whether I was eloquent and enjoyed

Admiration in society — and
I wonder whether I was bound in chains
And whipped to do a master's work who thought
Me less important than his horse — and I

Wonder whether in playing with words in
Becoming vigorous with exercise
In being compassionate with people
In walking with dignity in modest

Circumstances — I wonder whether I've
Done enough to sanctify this lifetime.

I am creating
momentum as my bodies
dissolve and arise
again and I'd like to think
I'm surfing inspiration.

Thunder before dawn is a drum without
Melody and lightning is a crack in
The dark revealing a fracture in the
Sky at odds with the sounding of the rain

On the roof that lulls and soothes and I'm not
Awake and not asleep but in a trance
Of childlike wonder absorbing the force
Of the night unpredictable and sharp

With clamor and fire as if I'm on the
Edge of battle and doom were in the air
As if violence were imminent and
The covers and the roof aren't protection

As if nothing could shield me from the spears
And the animosity of strangers.

There's not a hint of
my childish fear this morning
as the day is bright
and all that's left of the night
are puddles reflecting sky.

My head is an oven and the heat is
On and kernels of possibility
Are baking and one by one a thought will
Pop in my mind and off I go having

Gained a direction and while talking to
A friend anything I hear will ping a
Response and we will be ponging along
Together and if we have similar

Kernels we'll be popping excitedly
But when I'm in a group I find my mind
Will slip away and I will be searching
For beautiful women nearby because

I have seeds of loneliness baking and
Exploding controlling my direction.

Not one idea
is isolated as each
thought arises from
previous thoughts and I want
to have healthy direction.

In memory there are phantoms as I
Remember how I choose to remember
As I'm not choosing consciously as my
Dreaming personality is making

Choices as my experience is full
Of exquisite detail and today I
Am using an edited version of
Who I think I am — it is easy to

Remember difficulty and failure
But I need a gentle persistence to
Empty negative memories and to
Settle myself on a firm foundation —

While I'm sitting in the lotus posture
I know my heart is as vast as the sky.

The little me is
competing and criticizing
but the big me is
absorbing experience
and transforming.

I remember walking with Joshua
And becoming frustrated with his one
Word responses as he was refusing
To communicate as he was angry

And discouraged as he was putting me
At a distance as never before and
As a dad I wanted to help but I
Couldn't fathom the desperation I

Sensed in him and I didn't know whether
The mood was temporary was teenage
Angst or whether his difficulty was
Dangerous that needed my attention

And as I remembered the brilliant and
Carefree child I didn't know what to do.

I was proud of my
intelligent and cheerful
son but something was
happening and I wondered
am I doing something wrong?

It was a little odd that she would want
To go to Minneapolis to the
Asian food store for a final time the
Day before she had determined to board

A plane bound for her homeland in Japan
After the divorce was certified and
After a twenty-seven marriage
Dissolved because she said there were items

I would need but I discovered that she
Wanted to sit in the back seat and cry
And exercise her anger a final
Time while I drove forty minutes there and

Forty minutes back while I listened to
Music because what else could I have done?

It was her habit
to express frustration with
accusation and
tears and usually I
became quiet and distant.

Because Yoshiko's Dad repeatedly
Took his employers' money and lost it
Gambling on horse races — because her dad
Inherited compulsivity from

I don't know how many generations
Of misery — and because I arrived
In Japan young and ignorant as an
Alcoholic sober for only two

Years — Yoshiko and I were caught in a
Current and we didn't know where we were
Going as we were drawn together as
Her disturbed energy attracted me

As her pattern of behavior was like
A whirlpool circling a black hole.

Yoshiko's anger
escalated exploded
periodically
but I didn't understand
and I believed I caused it.

The rules of a family are established
By force of personality and no
One could get angrier and be angry
Longer than Yoshiko as she set the

Pattern of normalcy and eruption
As it was normal between explosions
To believe everything was OK and
I was proud of being married with kids

And after the anger she was kind and
Busy as long as possible until
Darkness emerged again and she lifted
Her blame shield that allowed her to find fault

Outside herself because it was too hard
To remember painful experience.

Even with sober
friends and meditation I
sometimes didn't know
if I were wrong or right as
we were in a world of hurt.

In a hotel room after her dad took
His employer's money again — after
He spent it at the racetrack — after she
Was married and pregnant — after angry

Managers came looking for payback from
Her and me — Yoshiko arranged to meet
Her Dad to tell him — like her mother and
Sister before her — that she had enough —

This was last time she wanted to see
Him and she wanted no contact and I
Remember how matter-of-fact she was
And I know there was no future contact

And I was a witness after we moved
To America word came he was dead.

We heard he died once
and we heard he died again
in mysterious
circumstances and we
heard he had died in squalor.

Memories are funny as they're buried
Within the mind and I wonder whether
Memories can poison the body as
Yoshiko endured diabetes and

Cancer and I wonder whether she and
Joshua could find solace as I do
In meditation because it seems that
Haphazard forgetting is like trying

To force water uphill and I'd like them
To talk about the phantoms whispering
In their heads I'd like them to understand
Clarity is necessary as I

Have learned to use the lotus position
To let memories arise and vanish.

In meditation
I face phantoms quietly
I let them go as
often as necessary
for acceptance to arise.

After thirty years of sitting in the
Lotus position with my spine straight and
My shoulders relaxed I've practiced breathing
And letting go of thoughts and I like the

Word liberation and I ponder what
It means and pondering is helpful as
I've filtered my memories and my fears
With the magic of peaceful consciousness

But pondering is not enough because
My mind is a bowl and I have to burn
Dispiriting thoughts and have to return
To emptiness as much as possible —

I can be peacefully awake because
I practice letting go of disturbance.

I don't have to rush
into tomorrow in an
effort to escape
yesterday I can take my
time and enjoy my breathing.

I allow my emotions to come and
Go and I understand more about why
Things happened as they did and why I got
Caught in patterns of circumstances but

While I watch the sun touch cottonwood leaves
I'm watching the sun and leaves apart from
Yesterday separate from tomorrow
As there are only leaves tinged with the light

Turning in a breeze and who could want more
And going about my business if I
Stumble into trouble I remember
I can appreciate my breathing as

I have discovered liberation means
Finding simplicity without demands.

In Buddhist sayings
this moment is the one bright
jewel dissolving
time and circumstance and I
have perfect freedom of choice.

Looking back on my time riding buses
On University Avenue from
St. Paul to Minneapolis and back
I remember feeling separate from

Everyone so I speculated on
What people did in the passing buildings
And I took glimpses of faces postures
And different ethnicities and I made

Up stories because I was so young and
Inexperienced and I had no sense
Of direction and I wanted to pierce
Surface appearances and I wanted

To explore the possibilities
But I wasn't ready to open doors.

I took pleasure in
reading philosophy on
austere winter nights
in the warmth of the bus and
no one interrupted me.

Youthful Ambition

I remember taking a bus downtown
With a pen a notebook and a sense of
Mission and I bought a cup of coffee
And I ascended the steps to the Saint

Paul Public Library and I saw the
Stone magnificence and I imagined
The Athenian Acropolis and
I dreamed that my destination was the

Parthenon and I sat in a quiet
Corner under a high ceiling amid
Marble columns with the poet John Keats
On my mind and I marshaled my focus

Because I was determined not to leave
Before I'd written a worthy sonnet.

I fidgeted
I drank coffee
I looked around
at the marble columns but
inspiration escaped me.

Facing a window and television
With the same sportscasters bloviating
At the same time everyday (whom I can't
Hear) there is the elliptical machine

At the gym that I fear and loath because
It draws me and makes me feel cowardly
If I don't get on — and I run like a
Lusty devil for thirty minutes and

I use headphones and music on my cell
Phone for motivation and distraction
And I follow a red dot circling
A racetrack and I watch a timer and

I run through the minutes and rush to a
Crescendo pushing on to exhaustion.

Whether lean or plump
gracefully or awkwardly
many of us are
making circular motions
while not traveling an inch.

St. Croix Crossing Bridge

The designs were contested for fifty
Years because the St. Croix River is a
National treasure that must be preserved —
And the beauty of the limestone bluffs and

The sinuous lines of the serpentine
Valley were taken into account — and
I watched for three years as vast portions of
The earth were repositioned and I heard the

The hammering of the earth making holes
From which the piers were raised and I saw the
Sections of the bridge hanging in air and
Day after day construction continued

And now the valley is refashioned with
The magic of wire rebar and concrete.

The old-fashioned lift
bridge in Stillwater
will be connected
to the Crossing Bridge
with a hiker's trail.

Utopia

Once the idea was accepted that
All means necessary should be taken
For the protection of the earth with the
Support of technological magic

Designers could offer proposals based
On equality and harmony so
Many thousands could live in a single
Sky Tower and the magnificence of

A building in which everyone would be
Given everything necessary and
The elegance of the suggestion that
People would rise above their squabbles and

Hardships to live peacefully in the clouds
Who could resist the enthusiasm?

Designers would need
to discourage obvious
comparisons with
beehives and ant colonies —
who would choose to be a drone?

The idea supporting Sky Towers
Is love of nature and the knowledge that
People tend to despoil the earth so in
Devotion to Gaia people would be

Willing to minimize their destruction
And gather together and the walls of
Their rooms could be pixilated with views
Of a forest a prairie a mountain

And the sensations of outdoors could be
Recreated with the seasons with sun
And stars and frogs in spring and crickets in
The summer nights and there would be no need

For people to roam about the landscape
And everyone could be safe and happy.

And the designers
could monitor the movement
of many thousands
and we could all celebrate
a sky of changing colors.

I've been following descriptions in the
News of architectural miracles
Of towers of steel and glass extending
A mile in height amounting to cities

Containing homes businesses indoor parks
And entertainment centers and what a
Dream for designers of an expertly
Controlled community — but I'd prefer

To live on the ground listening to the
Peeper frogs again in the spring and a
Fountain and a collection of trees on
The eighty-first floor wouldn't be enough

And if there were birds sequestered within
Steel and glass they would be a mockery.

A mile high tower
would make a lovely target
for a terrorist —
with ingenuity he
could detonate a city.

If people chose to live in Sky Towers
The designers would have discretion to
Apportion living space by applying
Flexible standards according to the

Population's preferences and perhaps
An equal distribution of room would
Prevail regardless of merit but some
Would have sunlight and scenery and some

Would live in boxes — some would be high and
Some low and as the disparity of
Property could be narrowed quality
Of life issues would remain because in

Comparison some people always do
Finagle better than most of us can.

How many things do
people really need and if
constrained within a
limited space wouldn't we
be happy with less clutter?

Even though people could be cloistered in
Sky Towers some would refuse to be —
Minerals would continue to be mined
And oil would be drilled and piped and with

The best technology the earth would be
Farmed and the animals slaughtered for our
Consumption — so it's dubious that the
Designers would establish a perfect

Separation of people and nature
But once the bulk of humanity sees
The wisdom of cooperation it's
Possible that we could achieve the dream

Of sustainable communities and
Limit contamination of the Earth.

Because it won't do
to have everyone doing
just as they please — we
need to assure our children
will have oxygen to breathe.

Stripping everything away at bottom
I'm a pink creature with appendages
And when I slide within the curtain and
Step into the shower entering the

Cascading warmth I reacquaint myself
With the bare facts without embarrassment
As if I were apart from scrutiny
As if I were Adam in Paradise

And while soaping and shampooing I watch the
Acrobatics of my thinking as I
Indulge complaints exult successes or
Wallow in guilt and nowhere else am I

As childlike as I am in the shower
Because I become me without armor.

Imagine stretching
yawning and removing
a bathrobe and
absentmindedly
entering Niagara Falls.

Grapes become
the voluptuous girl
luster becoming lust.

— *Tekkan*

Everyday Mind V

A summer morning
fog is obscuring my way —
driving downhill to
meet my friends again in
my familiar Stillwater.

Where ever understanding arises
Ignorance retreats at least for a while
Perhaps because I don't know whether I'll
Remember what I've learned in my next life

Because I know that I'm strung as taut as
Guitar strings pegged at one end needing to
Succeed in business pinned at the other
Persistently feeling lonely pegged by

Middle age and pinned with modest income
And pinned with political views out of
Tune with the establishment and pegged to
A sense of mission and pinned to Buddhist

Compassion and pegged with partisanship
And I'd like to produce some harmony.

I wonder how much
of me I will inherit
with my next body —
will I be curious and
will I be meditating?

Dragon Fly

You are a puzzle piece you are a bug
Born and living underwater for years
You can migrate over the oceans and
With two sets of wings you can angle each

Wing separately allowing you to fly
Sideways and backwards quickly and you can
Hover and you are a predator with
Three hundred sixty degree vision that

Sees colors people can't imagine and
You follow a single bug in a swarm
Snatching and tearing off its wings and with
Serrated mandibles eating in air —

I've wondered why the mosquitoes exist
And it seems they're here for you to gobble.

I can learn about
your abilities I can
marvel over your
exquisite composition
but you can't comprehend me.

Dragonflies have been evolving over
Three hundred million years and their heads are
Wrap-around eyes that see all directions
And each eye has thirty thousand facets

And each facet creates its own image
That combines into vision that gauges
Movement and sees colors beyond human
Capability making them super

Predators that can snatch a fly in flight
That can tear the fly's wings off and hold the
Fly in air with its legs while the dragon-
Fly is hovering with its four wings while
The dragonfly is cutting the fly in bits

By slicing with serrated mandibles —
But I don't believe it has emotions.

Imagine people
with wrap-around eyes instead
of faces — could we
gauge each other's emotions
could we fall in love?

If I could see as a dragonfly does
If I could see a mountain range with the
Rainbow spectrum a dragonfly does I'd
Marvel at the mountains the sun and the

Flowing clouds I'd appreciate beauty
But such colors don't exist for me and
I suppose in the mentality of
A dragonfly beauty has no purpose

And as a fly has no vocal cords it
Doesn't scream as a dragonfly rips off
Its wings so I wonder whether it knows
Horror as people do because people

Are capable of bug ferocity
Sometimes without a smidgen of regret.

Time runs off in both
directions — evolution
designs exquisite
killing machines — and yet I
take heart because of beauty.

The dragonfly has everything it needs
To be a dragonfly meaning it needs
Colors that I can't imagine meaning
There are aspects of reality I

Can't imagine and I don't imagine
A dragonfly needs sentiment as I
Use sentiment so the dragonfly needs
A spectrum of colors while I employ

A spectrum of emotions that makes me
Speculate about a superior
Consciousness with a wider array of
Emotions a deeper intelligence

I can't imagine and I wonder what
Such busy intelligence is doing?

I know just enough
to want to know more to need
to know more but if
it's unimaginable
which direction do I go?

Lascaux Caves

Cave art in France from seventeen thousand
Years ago is pregnant with hints as the
Bison horses and lions together
Are believed to be on the plains and the

Bulls horses deer and bears are supposed to
Be in forest and there is an ibex
A rhinoceros a feline apart
And artists used scaffolding to reach the

Ceilings and they prized yellow red and black
And they swabbed and blotted and sprayed with a
Tube and even as we stand where they stood
Their language is dissipated but were

They moved to create by desire and
Pride by their dreaming or perhaps pleasure?

Fire in the cave
illuminated rock
and generations
collaborated in
recreating life.

Carbon dating the tools pointed to the
Paleolithic era but the age
Of the art can not be determined and
Animals predominate but trees — and

Grass aren't depicted — and we've given names
To the Nave the Apse the Hall of Bulls and
The Chamber of Felines — but we don't know
The words they spoke — but the bulls and bison

Are stamping the horses' hooves are pounding
An archer is thrusting a knee forward
Confronting a line of deer charging and
The life presented bespeaks a throbbing

Heart and surging blood — but their manner of
Greeting and courtesy have disappeared.

Light and breath coming
with tourists introduced
fungus and black mold
so scientists are striving
to contain the corruption.

The camera on the craft Voyager One
Was turned around for a final shot of
The earth four billion miles behind as it
Proceeded to interstellar space and

Once the photo arrived it was filtered
And magnified and in a ray of light
Earth appeared as a pale blue dot prompting
The cosmologist Carl Sagan to

Say every human — ever — lived on a
Mote of dust suspended in a sunbeam
And he considers the poignancy and
The belittlement of human conceit —

Perhaps the miracle of consciousness
Could be explained with more than five senses.

We are spheres of
consciousness extending
only so far and
becoming aware of
vast ignorance.

Nothingness is a thing that's hard to grasp
As I close my eyes and sample blindness
And put fingers in my ears and pretend
To be deaf and a question emerges

Somehow vision became necessary
And the universe created eyesight
Sometime hearing became important and
And ears appeared to drink in sounds and I

Wonder whether the stars and sight arose
Simultaneously and where they came
From — anyway it's easy to marvel
At the flying of a bee humming bird

Putting a beak in a red blossom and
Comprehend exquisite vitality.

Everywhere I turn
I can see iridescence
and hear symphonies
but I also grow weary
and forget about beauty.

Total Solar Eclipse

Even though the differences in size and
The distances involved are understood
And the force of gravity propelling
The moon and earth about each other and

Around the sun is accurately known
And even though we know nowhere else in
The solar system do the orbs align
So much like hand and glove for the moon to

So exactly block the sun in passing
With just a rim of light escaping — the
Miracle is that waves of photons flow
In space into the biology of

The eye and somehow sight and consciousness
Come together and comprehend the facts.

For me seeing the
sunlight passing through
cottonwood leaves and
making me happy
is a miracle.

It's not obvious because the view from
Inside my head and my experience
And my secret thinking convince me of
My individuality and of

My boundaries but from a another point
Of view I can see we are a creature
With billions of eyes with a life spanning
Millennia as we have risen from

Living in caves to Sky Towers as new
Discoveries are passed among us and
I can't predict our direction and my
Comprehension is a pinprick in the

Fabric of space/time but together the
Body of humanity is growing.

The predation
among people
is a disease that
hasn't quite killed us
as we are evolving.

While it's true my history is a trail
Of behavior that puts me here today
And it's true I'm faced with choices only
I can make and it's true my emotions

Resemble the focus of my world but
It's also true my emotions more or
Less aren't much different from my fellows'
And while I seem to be independent

From others I want to remember the
Words I'm using are common currency
And the wellspring of my motivations
Come from the people I admire and

My thoughts are amalgamations of
What other people communicated.

If I were alone
words would be useless
emotions would be
rudimentary
lacking refinement.

Tour de France

As if they were designing a rocket
With the intention of landing on the
Moon a subset of mechanics has been
Busy developing bicycles with

Cutting aerodynamics with feather
Weight with frictionless performance aiming
For continuous improvement over
The previous models because they are

Serving a species of athletes and a
Collection of enthusiasts who love
Bicycle races who love combining
The rigor of competition with the

Magic of evolving technology
Who love the pursuance of perfection.

The bicycle suits
are breathable stretchy and
light as a feather
flamboyantly colorful
wind cheating fashionable.

Some are tall and bulky and their muscles
And hearts are suited for the sprint to the
Finish and some are from high altitude
Nations and they are as slight as birds and

They specialize in ascending mountains
But the rider capable of winning
The three week race must be alert for the
Cross winds that can split groups of riders must

Know when to race and when to follow must
Climb the Alps well and must be able to
Assume the arrow posture of the time
Trial bike and race against the clock alone

Because to win the Tour de France he must
Master the sport with a will to triumph.

He must dedicate
himself to exertion
must leverage the
pinnacle of bodily
strength in turning pedals.

They know every inch of the mountains they
Climb because they scout the sharpest turns the
Grueling gradations and tucked in the back
Of their jerseys they have a radio

And with a headset they talk to the team
Manger about strategy and each
Rider of the team understands his role
In supporting the leader by lining

Up and conserving his energy with
A slipstream so he's ready at the right
Moment to launch himself to attack the
Strongest climbers of the day because the

Point of the team is to protect their best
Rider — his victory is their doing.

The corporations
funding the teams are aiming
to embed the names
of their companies in the
minds of a mass audience.

Teams of riders come with an entourage
Larger than rock bands with a chef a bus
And mechanics and throughout the race the
Riders are followed by team cars with a

Manager co-opting live videos
From the media to appraise himself
And direct his riders by radio
And if someone has a flat tire there are

Support cars with extra tires bikes and
Even shoes — and once Marcel Kittle fell
And needed a new bike while waiting and
Losing time and he busted a shoe too —

He was bruised bloody and impetuous
Changing shoes while pedaling with one leg.

There's no place for a
leading rider to hide on
the Tour de France and
fanatic dedication
precludes humiliation.

The race has become sophisticated
And the teams are lubricated machines
But riders must pedal themselves and the
Mountain slopes of the Pyrenees and Alps

Loom over each rider as there are days
Of ascending three mountains a day and
Each rider must turn the corners of the
Roads and keep pace with the best dancing on

Pedals and everyone tries not to crack
But when descending everyone tests the
End of courage as there's no protection
From harrowing speed from challenging turns

From bone shattering falls apart from the
Perfection of aerodynamic skill.

The bicycles are
fifteen pound machines
and the riders are
flesh and blood athletes
overcoming mountains.

Sprinters are bulky and not suited for
The mountain stages but they must finish
Within a time limit and there are days
Of meandering in sunflowers cornfields

And lavender or along the coast in
The morning in the afternoon when the
Peloton doesn't hurry until it's
Time to organize as teams form in lines

As distance to the finish is measured
And a rapid tempo is established
And sprinters conserve energy within
A slipstream and the leadout men peel off

One by one as positioning happens —
And the winner sprints across in a blur.

Eight hours of racing
two hundred kilometers
come down to fractions
of inches as position
at the end is critical.

Almost every day a group of riders
Breaks away early from the peloton
Stretching a lead to ten minutes and these
Riders from the rival teams need to work

Together each one taking a turn in
Front slicing wind for the others because
Such a small group will soon exhaust itself
As the peloton keeps grinding on and

Almost always the peloton decides
To organize in a line and run down
The rebels and they almost always do
As one by one insurgents crack but some

Days because of timing or terrain or
Cussedness a breakaway hero wins.

Winning a stage of
the glorious affair takes
teamwork even with
rival riders up until
the final fifty meters.

There's a green jersey awarded to the
Rider winning sprints and polka-dot for
Winning mountains and white for the best young
Rider but yellow goes with the fastest

Accumulating time requiring
Leaders to be masters of strategy
Speedy in the solitary racing
Of time trials and dancers up the mountains

Because the one with the yellow jersey
Must be consistently at the front in
Rain and over cobblestones and after
A fall and he must be in the leading

Group split by a crosswind because winning
For three weeks is a difference of seconds.

Racers are handed
bars of nutrition in eight
hours of racing and
everyone sometimes has to
take a pee behind a tree.

Watching the tour on T.V. on the couch
Is the pinnacle of summer splendor
For me as riders sweat up the Alps and
Pelt down gargantuan slopes and pedal

Between fields of sunflowers and follow
Streams in and out of shady trees and grace
Medieval castles and manors along
The way and I don't have to schlep up a

Mountain myself and wait all day to watch
Them pass just once but I can drink coffee
And listen to expert commentary
While sitting on a cushion as they take

The final laps on the Champs-Elysees
After weeks of toil — and sprint to the end.

As the caffeine
circulates in my blood
and my heart beats
a healthy rhythm
I am participating.

I remember the navy blue jerseys
Of the U.S. Postal riders in line
Protecting Lance Armstrong on the mountains
On the plains as he won the Tour de France

For the seventh time and I remember
His teammate Floyd Landis winning a Tour
Too but the glory dissolved when Floyd was
Caught breaking rules by taking drugs and in

Bitterness Floyd revealed that Lance and his
Team were cheats also as they were using
Performance boosting drugs every year of
Every victory as they devised tricks

To evade the tests as cheating was just
Another necessary skill to win.

Once there's cheating
once cheaters win
how can riders
compete without
competing?

I Am Bumble

Some people are asking why I'm calling
Myself Bumble and I say I like the
Buoyant "b"s surrounding the u and m
Because it sounds as if the two "b"s are

Stretching the string of a bass guitar and
When enunciating Bumble the umm
Arises in air reverberating
And warming my tummy and it isn't

So long as to seem grandiloquent but
Its briefness is pithy even puckish
And it's not a name that's commonly heard
So it's unlikely to be forgotten

Easily and I like the idea
Of people saying look here comes Bumble.

Saying names is
a call and response
game and I'm
introducing
variety.

I can do so many things with my phone
Like send email and read the news on the
Internet and listen to music while
Exercising but I especially

Depend on the navigation system
When going somewhere new on the highway
And there are settings within my app where
I can select the shortest or the least

Congested route but I don't fool with the
Settings but there came a day when we were
Late on the way to a wedding and the
Robotic woman's voice sent us to a

Strip mall and told us we'd arrived but we
Were lost adrift and disoriented.

Maybe the snafu was
in the application or
the satellite or
the monotone woman was
just being emotional.

I was on my own with the cilantro
As I didn't know how much of the stems
To keep with the little leaves so I tore
The leaves from the stems with my fingers and

Put them in the bowl — and I cut into
A squishy mango and discovered it
Had a hard core but I finagled the
Knife and put squares of mango in the bowl —

And I was surprised that avocados
Also have a hard core but I chopped up
Four and put them in the bowl along with
A pineapple and green onions and one

Jalapeno pepper without the seeds —
And then I sprinkled on some lemon juice.

Everything was
an experiment
for my début at
David's summer salsa
extravaganza.

I would like to say I'm considerate
And capable of solving world weighty
Controversies but I'm more likely to
Scratch my chin while strategizing how

To get the attention of my friends — but I
Won't be critical because I know it's
Natural to linger smack dab in the
Middle of me — and while preparing for

David's salsa extravaganza I
Discovered mango and pineapple and
Blue berries go well together and adding
Cilantro green onions avocados

And lemon juice is marvelous and while
Stirring it all — my mind became the bowl.

On my own I would
be as likely to chew on
a cottonwood leaf
as a bunch of cilantro —
I don't know what's eatable.

Yesterday to meet a friend of my friend
I drove fifty miles to Menomonie
Wisconsin to Jake's Supper club where I've
Never been and I was rushing on the

Highway because time slips away from me
And I drank more coffee than I should and
Stopped at a rest room with an eye on my
Watch and I was excited not nervous

Because I was exploring because my
Friend created a shimmering image
In my head because I was turning a
Corner with joyful anticipation —

Sometimes reality is a bubble
Bursting and I readjust with a smile.

Adrenalin
possibility
anticipation
are fun before
revelation.

My smooth skin and glossy hair disappeared
A while ago and it can't be said I
Am tall and I wonder how my friend
Described me to his friend and whether when

I emerged a shimmering image of
Romeo popped like a bubble and it's
Unfortunate because once the bubble
Bursts the fun of imagination is

Gone and reality bites but when I
Remember how much I didn't know and
How sloppy my attitudes were when I
Was young and when I see how age turns each

Of us into worn shoes I'm grateful my
Experience allows me to listen.

Words and stories
reveal whether
experience
was enlightening
or a waste of time.

Her mother was cremated in June and
Family and friends assembled for a
Ceremony at the cemetery
And a little box was put in the ground

And before the hole was recovered with
Dirt Marina put a book — the same book
Her mother read to Marina before
Sleeping — next to the box in the hole and

In October while Marina was in
The passenger's seat of an ambulance
While she was doing her best to rescue
Others there was an accident on the

Highway and Marina full of life was
Killed and it just doesn't seem possible.

Marina
eager and
cheerful
is gone.

Saturday morning is like the first day
Of vacation for me because I free
Myself from the demands of absorbing
And manipulating information

Of serving a partisan readership
Who are expecting affirmation and
Insight — but on Saturday morning I
Forget about my mission and cavort

And I don't have to impose opinions
And it's not necessary to be right
And I enjoy my friends whatever they are
Thinking because we gather to pursue

In meditation — quiet extending
In all directions — in-between thinking.

The quiet flows
continuously
and it's seldom
as demanding as
the past or future.

It's never been so crowded as I stood
Half in and out of the door waiting in
Line at the coffee shop on Saturday
Morning after mediation but I

Didn't mind because our Zen contingent
However slowly was advancing and
Mixing with others we didn't know and
I enjoy watching people — anyway

After a session of practiced quiet
Gabbing comes naturally and today
Paul captivated conversation by
Telling a story about scouting in

A town of secretive polygamists —
Who could predict such a turn of events?

Pouring caffeine on
top of meditation is
a wonderful way
to finish off a Saturday
morning — who knows what's coming?

I was given a pair of castoff clogs
In the spring and they're a smidgen big for
Me but I love the ease of slipping them
On and I don't have to bend over and

I only have to stick my feet in and they
Are so like a pair of slippers with an
Inch and a half soles that give me that much
More stature and once summer arrived I

Stopped wearing socks and I'm celebrating
The season by also wearing the most
Colorful silk shirts while typing these words
In my short pants with my knees bent and with

My feet arched and my naked heels up
Luxuriating in the summer air.

Once in a while a
little stone will find its
way under my foot
so I raise my toes and it
falls from my clog easily.

Each of us has a special conception
Of entertainment and nutrition and
Of what's appropriate for us and I'm
Grateful because he's helping out around

The house as he spots movement and follows
With his eyes as his ears go forward as
He tenses and springs and scrambles and swipes
And lunges and paws as well as he can

And I'd say he's as limber and precise
As a ballerina but he's frantic
In pursuit with not a hint of grace or
Discipline and he's pleasure to watch —

None of the others could do what he did
As Kit Cat caught and ate the nuisance fly.

Which was better
catching or eating
the fly — I
couldn't do it not
without seasoning.

Kit Cat is a miniature mountain lion
And after eating he ignites and jumps
On the refrigerator and gallops
In the house and wrestles with Johnnie as

Johnnie flops on his back and keeps Kit at
Bay with his legs — and everyday Kit Cat
Assumes the role of supremo but I
Was puzzled to see Kit's ears were scabby

And I couldn't guess how he came by his
Wounds until I saw Johnnie on his back
Kicking with his hinds legs at Kit's face as
Kits was reaching for a part of Johnnie

To bite but Johnnie wiggled and twisted
And nailed until Kit Cat strutted away.

Kit is a cat of
commotion and nerve
and Johnnie is
watchful quiet and
full of surprises.

Hi — I'm bloviation alcoholic
So don't pay much attention to me as
I get a kick listening to myself
As you suspect a lack of substance in

My words but communication is how
I keep from drinking so please indulge a
Little gas as I think the future is
Not what we suppose but does resemble

A tiger jumping from behind and we
Don't know what's coming and often we
Are not prepared and the past doesn't trail
Behind us but is everywhere before

Us and we just can't stop remembering
And what we remember isn't healthy.

A sober drunk
may be sensitive
and self-conscious
and with sobriety
may become vainglorious.

Cancer is a tiger pouncing on an
Unsuspecting soul from behind and it
Doesn't happen to everyone all at
Once but one by one and the division

Between observing and getting sick is
Like being on a body of water
On the periphery of a whirlpool
And proximity is an illusion

As over time everyone encounters
The deadly circular current leading
To the abyss as far as we know but
Mixing with the preponderance of fear

Is the potential for growing a heart
Emanating the gift of compassion.

We can't seem to do
without enduring fear but
buried within is
also a capacity
for growing compassion.

I've grown accustomed to bearing the load
Of living with people as I'm paying
The mortgage the car and the telephone
Bills and car insurance is sensible

But health insurance is a government
Racket so I'm doing without it and
I'm familiar with the summer lull and
Autumn resurgence of cash coming in

Peculiar to my business and this year
I'm working around a tax penalty
Due to a late payment and I'm learning
How to put my financial concerns in

A box in my mind as I'm doing my
Daily routine helping me feel normal.

So many people
need to be paid and
most of them I don't
know but I'm the same —
I need to be paid.

The dog days of summer never came this
Year as the air was clear and mild and now
It's already chilly at sunrise and
Twilight — near the ending of August — and

This morning I see the foliage of trees
In Stillwater is barely stirring and
There's not a single bird under a sky
Heavy with grayish clouds gradually

Disappearing — but I don't care because
By this afternoon I'll be driving in
Town with the windows open and I'll be
Walking in my short pants feeling the warmth

Of the sun on my bare legs — I don't have
The time to think about cold days coming.

There are hints of
bare trees and
lacerating wind
I'd rather not
think about.

Plato's Cave

I was dreaming and facing the rock wall
Of a cave chained and unable to turn
To see the fire behind me and all
I could see were the shadows of people

Dancing on the illuminated stone
Before me and I felt the weight of my
Slavery and an urge of my body
Compelled me to rise from bed and stumble

To the bathroom to pee while I was half
Dreaming and half awake marveling in
A twilight trance imprisoned but wanting
To escape my ignorance to break the

Chains and emerge from the depth into the
Sunlight — where I could feel the wind flowing.

Plato believed the
visible world is only
an illusion and
what he called the ideals
exist beyond our grasping.

Mom found it in an envelope box while
Dusting bookshelves and I saw spots of age
On the cover as she hesitated —
Because I can be cranky — but this was

Dad's doctoral dissertation that he
Came to American to write as he
Wanted an education and in these
Pages remain his youthful pursuit of

A rational basis for faith and we
Knew the millennia of scholarship
The culmination of effort these typed
Words are as he tried so hard to be a

Messenger of wisdom and a leader
For people who were trying to be good.

Mom is a faithful
guardian of each issue
of fifty years of
publishing a journal that
Dad and I did together.

I remember pondering in autumn
The meaning of melancholy when I
Was young during my drinking days when I
Liked the twilight season in between the

Sunshine the rippling water and the
Wildflowers and the inescapable
Cold — because a drinker savors sadness —
And a turning from the light to gloom is

Familiar — but with the layering on
Of thirty years I've learned to savor the
Party colors of the leaves differently
As marks of time and reminders of

People and places disappearing like the
Leaves dissipating in a bracing wind.

I'm not savoring
notions of sadness
I'm remembering
what really was but
isn't any more.

I have to keep coming back — otherwise
I could resort to a bicycle or
A donkey — because this is what we do
To fill our tanks with gasoline because

I'm expected in St. Paul in forty
Minutes and calculating the distance
The stoplights the traffic the construction
On the highway I've got no time to waste

So here I am at Neighbor's Stop again
And soon I'll have to take my mittens off
Because they're too bulky and insert my
Credit card with freezing fingers and

Once the nozzle of the pump is in the
Car I watch the numbers of the price rocket.

The combustion of
gasoline speeds me over
distances as corn
fields and strip malls arise and
disappear before my eyes.

I see an apple tree in front of a
Modest home with crooked and trimmed branches
That's on my route to Bayport — and I've seen
It in February decorated with

Christmas bulbs providing a bleak season
With a little cheer — and in April in
Passing I've seen the apple blossoms
Reminding me of beauty — and in the

Summer it's easy to forget because
It's just a little tree among the more
Imposing trees — but this autumn I do
Remember it because I remember

Apples come from apple trees and nothing
Is better in autumn than ripe apples.

The Christmas bulbs
hung in the apple tree are
ornamental fruit —
but the apples in autumn
are natural fruition.

On the verge of September the sun is
Still a resplendent presence in the sky
And on the edge of sixty years of life
My body is phenomenal but the

Symptoms of asthma that I carry were
Triggered this year by the drifting smoke of
The wildfires in California and in
Oregon and my breath is constricting

And I'm lucky to have medicine and
I'm determined to work around tightness
Of breath when necessary and I don't
Think about my horizons very much

But at the pinnacle of my health I
Am reminded everything is passing.

Asphyxiation
wouldn't be much fun
but whatever
happens I'm looking for
continuing horizons.

I try to bring my thoughts down to a low
Simmer and if successful I'm aware
Of sights and sounds and so I've noticed while
Walking my left ankle pops sometimes and

So does my left index finger and if
I were in a funk I'd never hear how
Peculiar my bones can be but when I
Try to make my joints crack it doesn't work

So it's not possible to create a
Rhythmic jingle and I'm not even sure
Whether bone or cartilage snaps or
If humidity or temperature

Is responsible but I will listen
Carefully for the next permutation.

I suppose
big old Paul
has a bass knee
I have a tenor ankle.

The everyday world is coy while I go
About my business thinking about a
Dozen things I don't want to see blossom
Into problems but I escape pressure

By taking time in the morning to play
With words while I have clarity because
I so often do cross a threshold of
Satisfaction that carries me through the

Day but to keep playing I depend on
A split second of recognition when
I see something funny or worthy of
Remembering as a starting point so

Within the happenstance of everyday
I am a hunter of hidden marvels.

Inspiration came
in the church sanctuary
as we were quiet
walking and meditating
I heard my ankle snap.

At a gathering of my family
My mom reminded me of Louie our
Miniature black poodle we named after
A French King and I haven't thought of him

For fifty years and only my mom and
I knew Louie who had a high-pitched bark
Who wouldn't be quiet sometimes and we
Remembered how he sprang through the front door

When he could and my brother my sister
And I chased him as he ran in frantic
Circles pleased that he was free until he
Tired and it's funny how words can spark a

Memory and I'm back on a tree-lined
Boulevard within Hutchinson Kansas.

There's a place in my
head where Louie was waiting
to be remembered
and he's running in circles
again until I get tired.

Indian Summer

If I were to epitomize a day
Of my life saying this is what it feels
Like to be alive I suppose I could
Come close to an ideal by dwelling in

A September afternoon because as
I remember the air is often mild
And the sky is sunny and the clouds drift
Lazily and I'm comfortable in

A t-shirt and I could pick an apple
Off a tree and eat it and even as
The mornings and evenings are becoming
Chilly and the night is lengthening the

Warmth of a September afternoon makes
Me believe everything is provided.

The year always comes
around to a September
afternoon again
but I recognize comfort
is temporary.

Sometimes a diagnosis comes without
Possibility of recovery
With palliative care the only option
And I can't imagine how I would feel

If told of multiple lesions large and
Deep within my brain that brought the loss of
Coordination and concentration
As I'm sure I'd have premonitions but

The words coming from a doctor would be
A pronouncement of the end coming more
Quickly than expected but leaving time
Enough for preparations and choices —

With time enough to remember the good —
To compose myself — and to say goodbyes.

I think I've been
preparing for the
eventuality
of my transition
but I'm not ready.

I resolve to identify something
Worthy of remembering everyday
Whether it be a memory — like how
I heard a British student use the word

Worthy when I was in England and I
Realize I'm been imitating him
Ever since — or whether it be a way
Of seeing — like what would I do if I

Were given a dead end prognosis with
Little time left — because I believe so
Much of life slips by while I'm consumed
With trivialities — that I resolve

To calm my mind and to open my eyes
And identify something that's worthy.

Everyday
opportunity
rises with the sun —
something will be fresh
and I'll play with words.

The word tamongoes isn't accurate
As people call them tomatoes and what
Good is a word if people don't know it's
Meaning and I don't know why it came from

My mouth and maybe something is amiss
In my head but I like the sound of ta-
Mon- goes because it has an exotic
Flavor that makes me think of mangoes that

Have a hard core while the tomatoes are
Runny but both are sweet and juicy and
Both fit within my hand — anyway when
Some of us gathered around the table —

To look at what Lee brought to give away —
I liked the shock of saying tamongoes.

It's fun to defy
Expectations by
Behaving strangely —
When you say poodle
I'll say elephant.

Once caffeine enters the calculation
A peak and valley must be expected
And I do find myself attached to my
Morning cup of coffee — believing what's

The point of a sunrise without a boost
Of stimulation — and after sips and
A little time I am limber and am
Ready at my desk summoning the words —

Half of me becomes a receptive eye
Absorbing as much of my presence as
Possible and half of me becomes a
Response that rises from somewhere and if

I am especially nimble the words
Settle into place without confusion.

The force of my
concentration
opens a window —
opportunity
quickly dissipates.

Would it be beneficial to know what
People are thinking in the privacy
Of their heads while their expressions may show
Contentment or agreement would it help

Me to know with certainty whether they
Are bored and preoccupied with something
Not my business because it's enough for
Me to manage the promptings of my own

Thinking as I know my face and words do
Express a false front sometimes as I try
To be in harmony and the question
Whether it's necessary to be frank

Or better to be courteous is a
Choice that's an everyday predicament.

My impassive eyes
are watching carefully for
the subtlest clues
in your changing expressions —
just as you're watching me.

I feel the strain of keeping pace with the
World and meeting the expectations that
Come with my job and with the people in
My life as I depend on money and

Friendliness to go on and sometimes I
Get agitated thinking I'm cornered
By what people want from me and by what
I want that isn't happening and I'd

Like a different life but don't know what to
Do as I'm looking for direction and
Patience but even on a cloudy day
I notice the morning is beautiful

As I'm taking time and absorbing the
Covering of the mother-of-pearl clouds.

Sometimes I'd like to
jump out of myself
but where to go is
the conundrum so
I'll keep being me.

My Japanese Zen master expressed a
Quiet dignity not dependant on
What people thought of him because he was
Purposeful and he pointed to the need

In daily practice to forget the self
By mixing with the moment completely
And he would say if fearful be fearful
If irritated be irritated

And he didn't mean to be unkind to
People but he said it's important to
Experience the emotion clearly
To face difficulty without running

Because there is no separation from
What is and I would realize the truth.

Preoccupation
with self-criticism or
self-condemnation
is putting another head
on top of my working head.

And my Japanese Zen master said we
Americans need to learn to chew the
Words of masters more than we do because
Chewing aids the digestion and the words

"Study the self to forget the self to
Drop body and mind and be enlightened
By the myriad things" are said to be
Legitimate and worth considering

And he also said study the moment
And I've made a practice of attending
To whatever comes to mind as it comes
Without evasion because he said the

Forgetting of the self happens in an
Instant and can only happen right now.

Practice depends
on poise and
receptivity
even if emotion
has me in a grip.

A fog enveloped the trees and homes of
Stillwater before the sun rose and I
Saw only the shadows of things because
Of the street lights I passed while driving and

I loved the solitude and wanted to
Put my energy to use and it seemed
The fog represents the true face of the
World that over a familiar landscape

I've grown exhausted with if I depart
From my habitual activity
Uncertainty is pervasive and if
I keep my eyes open and attend to

What emerges new possibilities
Could present themselves if I am ready.

I believe the world
is pregnant with
possibility
but I've become
habituated.

I remember picking apples from a
Tree in the neighborhood when I was a
Kid and the skins were crisp and the fruit was
Fresh and juicy and all my life apples

Have never tasted as good as those when
I was roaming Bayport in a t-shirt
On a bicycle without a care — but
As I'm driving through Stillwater watching

The leaves blooming with color — I think of
Red and yellow apples and realize
It takes winter spring summer and fall to
Bring apples to fruition — and for me

Autumn becomes a juicy ripe apple —
A culmination of the shining sun.

As my rootedness
in years has brought me
understanding of
natural fruition
and its evanescence.

Photons are invisible scientists
Say and the brain exists in darkness yet
Somehow energy is flowing in the
Eyes the nerve cells the synapses and the

Visual cortex and somehow sunlight
And starlight reveal the vastness of the
Universe and the speed of light and space
Time has been calculated but there is

No explanation for how I have a mind
That sees and comprehends the miracle
Of my mother's motherly concern for
Her gladioli and geraniums

And chrysanthemums that expresses a
Nurturance underlying everything.

Consciousness expands
until it bumps against its
limitations and
devolves to geraniums
and chrysanthemums.

I blinked with realization after
I forgot to file my business taxes
So I raced to my accountant and we
Filed quickly and then I received a

Notice from the I.R.S. demanding
A thousand dollars and my accountant
Said taxes weren't owed and he'd write a
Letter and the penalty wouldn't stick

But I received another letter and
I considered why my signature was
Necessary just to prove I'd read it
And then I discovered two weeks warning —

They will break my door and seize property
Unless I pay a thousand dollars fast.

Sometimes I find
visions come to mind
and I'm seeing
I.R.S. agents
falling from airplanes.

I saw some teenage boys haggling on
The street as they were organizing a
Game with a ball and bat that led me to
Remember how boys will argue and shout

How aggression determines dominance
And the pack apportions the status of
Each and I remember my brother and
I roamed the neighborhood on bicycles

And we joined the other boys in games of
Football and baseball in empty lots and
We knew the rules because we watched the pros
Who were gods in stadiums on T.V. —

And I remember Harmon Killebrew
Swinging his bat for another home run.

I remember
Tony Oliva
running and stretching
for a long fly ball —
perfectly graceful.

I would like to thank my friend for showing
Me how easily my ego bruises
On Saturday morning — even after
Meditation — when we gathered at the

Coffee shop at our usual table
As I thought we were having a lively
Discussion and I was insightful and
He was looking at me and listening

But then he responded to someone else
Revealing he was looking at me but
Attending to others and it took a
Little time to laugh at myself because

I do exactly the same thing and need
To practice lessening my importance.

It's a burden to
be needy of attention
when people are
already accepting me
and what more do I want?

Sometimes the moon is big and other times
Small and it may look orange or silver
Depending on circumstances and on
My own I wouldn't understand but I

Know its orbit is elliptical so it
Comes closer to and farther from the earth
And I know on average it's about
Twenty thousand miles away because I

Discovered the facts on the Internet
And I've learned the moon's gravity keeps the
Earth from wobbling and thereby we have
Reliable seasons and I think it's

Marvelous we live with a burning sun
An orbiting moon and ripe tomatoes.

The sun is ninety-
three million miles
away and I am
happy it is not
nearer or further.

The Bench Press

It was a thing I happened upon that
Set me apart from others that gave me
Encouragement that I could lay on my
Back and lower a heavy barbell and

Successfully lift it when most other
Teenagers couldn't that got me into
Wrestling that got me used to life long
Exercise that gave me a goal in my

Thirties to press three hundred pounds while I
Weighed one hundred and forty that I worked
Hard to accomplish and one day I got
The bar half-way up a little higher

On the left side which was always stronger
And I came close but finally couldn't.

I trained as hard as
possible and took my shot
and afterwards I
knew my opportunity
was vanishing with time.

There is a constant ringing in my ears
That I notice when I choose to notice
And for years I meditated while in
The bedroom next to mine Joshua was

Playing video games with who knows whom
On the web and making electronic
Racket but I got good at not hearing
Nuisance noise — though I did have to shut him

Up whenever he was swearing — but then
Once I settle within my posture an
Energy arises and everyday
I discover the magic of focus —

Consciousness perpetuates energy
And there's no telling where I am going.

A black zafuton
and a black zafu
filled with buckwheat
are my connection
to the universe.

I sit on the edge of turbulence and
Serenity and find that silence is
Theoretical as there is always
A dog barking and traffic humming in

The distance just as nothingness is an
Idea hard to wrap my arms around
And while I'm teetering on the edge my
Attention has to go somewhere and it's

Impossible to banish sensations
And I can't often predict when a thought
Will give rise to a line of thinking that
Will be difficult to dislodge without

Effort but whatever comes to mind I
Practice watching the moment being.

A lot can happen
in forty minutes
even though I am
not moving — my mind
is hovering.

I was attracted to a type of the
Silk shirts at the thrift store and bought about
A dozen and a friend pronounced the name
Of the style but I didn't catch the word

And was too embarrassed to admit my
Ignorance within the circle of my
Friends but I understood that the style was
Cuban so I called them my garbanzo

Shirts for a joke to prompt my friend to say
Guayabera again and that's how I
Got the name and that's how I discovered
A joker can get away with a lot —

But I must admit I really didn't
know the meaning of garbanzo either.

I thought garbanzo
was an appellation for
a mafia goon
and I was being clever
until I looked up the word.

I'm not pretending to be the smartest
Or the wisest but I enjoy playing
With words because I find satisfaction
In constructing little lines of words and

In stacking them upon each other to
Make walls of words that serve as pictures of
Moments in a life and it's possible
To clarify what experience means

And today I find autumn has many
Voluptuous connotations as the
The occasion of ripe tomatoes and
Apples and suddenly the leaves are

Are on fire with color on the days of
Indian summer before winter comes.

It's fun to be
spontaneous
as I grasp at
geese fixing them in
v formations.

Autumn is dissolving again as leaves
Are scattered on the ground crumpled and brown
And this morning I see leaves collecting
With the rain spattering in the puddles

Along the street and I am watching the
Sweeping of the wipers clearing the rain
From my windshield allowing me to see
Autumn dissolving again as I go

To meet friends again as I do every
Morning regardless of the season as
My routine is my stability and
I often go to the same place at the

Same time to see familiar faces and
Laugh as autumn is dissolving again.

I drink coffee and
am perky in the
morning in every
season as my blood
is circulating.

Who could blame Mr. Bean for snoozing in
His folding chair while he was alone in
An empty museum in uniform
As a security guard puffing with

His lips fluttering and then his back slipped
Down the metal chair and he almost slid
Out of the chair while his mouth was open
And then he bent forward with his chest just

About touching his knees and he wavered
On the edge of the chair on the verge of
Collapse but he found a precarious
Point of balance and then he snorted and

Startled and rose back into the chair with
His arms dangling and he was still asleep.

Mr. Bean was
a human noodle
who gave himself to
child-like foolishness
to make people laugh.

Equinox

This is not the end as there is no end
But the harvest moon this October is
A symbol for me of the frictionless
Motion of the orb that functions as a

Mirror for the sun that is a marker
For the equal division of day and
Night on a predictable schedule as
A balancing of sunlight and starlight

I appreciate — and I see crumpled
Leaves on the grass with the light of an
Orange moon as round as a pumpkin
As it rises in twilight and becomes quite

Stunning transforming into a silver
Luminous moon traveling in the night

Chinese poets
centuries ago
left traces of
themselves with words of
moonshine Zen and wine.

Circles of Sober Alcoholics

Come with a story and take your turn as
One of us welcome within the circle
Meeting every morning for an hour and
When we're done we'll disperse to our lives with

A renewed sense of purpose because it's
Not about beating the obsession with
Alcohol for most of us but about
Living differently finding confidence

Discovering the inspiration to
Be useful and productive and once in
A while I'm pleasantly surprised because
I realize how much I've changed from the

Miserable drunk with a splitting head
To an optimist exploring today.

It's our purpose with
stories to encourage those
obsessed with drinking
to show it's possible to
overcome the urge to drink.

I know a guy on a spiritual path
Meaning he's trying to be sober and
On the night of a lunar eclipse he
Resolved to take the time to watch as a

Shadow passed across the moon because he
He thought seeing the event would make him
Happy and he persevered until the
Moon appeared again full and luminous

But he was disappointed because he
Invested his time and effort because
He couldn't see himself as we see him
Grasping for the moon and being silly

As emotions come and go and it takes
Time to learn that emotions come and go.

The moon is
in the heart and
a passing shadow
takes its time but
the moon is in the heart.

Ordinary or trivial is how
He imagines the lives of most people
Believing perhaps there's not much to be
Discovered or inspired by as he's

A lawyer and routinely meets people
At their unhappiest and as he's just
A little cynical and talks about
Changing his profession I think he's snared —

I wish him greater dissatisfaction
He's not unhappy enough to pursue
The wholehearted search for inspiration
As loneliness cuts away illusions

As urgency sharpens perception as
Intuition arises he'd transform.

Sleeplessness helped me
pay attention to my thoughts
restlessness pushed me
to seek something meaningful
providing satisfaction.

Did you learn to swallow emotion as
You drank and did your drinking assume a
Mysterious compulsiveness crossing
Boundaries and making limitations

Of time or quantity laughable and
Did the drinking come to a horrible
End and a tenuous ambivalent
Sobriety — And have you discovered

A mysterious division between
Everyday events and your emotions
As if you were a troubled child learning
About anger for the first time — to be

Sober it's necessary to face the
Emotions you evaded through the years.

Sobriety is
the barest beginning of
a new way of life —
once anger is surrendered
forgiving is natural.

It's not the first time he's been acknowledged
For staying sober for a length of time
And it's our custom to give medallions
Signifying the months or years and to

Hear from him about how sobriety
Was achieved — and so he tells a story —
And as we go around the circle and
Everyone has a say we cheer him with

Stories and you may not comprehend our
Happiness — he has a bowl of six-month
Medallions and thinks he should return them
Perhaps being confused about failure

And success as he sees only the months
While we appreciate the many years.

We remind ourselves
we have a mission to do
not to drink today
and if there is only shame
there's no room for saving grace.

We haven't seen her for months and it's so
Predictable that she would say as she
Did say that she intends to come again
Regularly and we know that as she's

Saying the words she really means it and
Yes it is possible in a moment
To make a resolution and to be
Sober going forward but we also

Know that saying the words is not enough —
It takes an unbearable amount of
Pain to stay quit before the obsession
To drink and some of us never seem to

Cross the mysterious threshold within
And surrender to God and become safe.

To be one of us
to be one who doesn't drink —
it's not about pride
it's about surrendering
and opening completely.

It's a curious blindness that he can't
Appreciate the gift he gave us in
Speaking truthfully about the abuse
He suffered at the hands of his family

That he would reveal the hole in his soul
That no subsequent accomplishment could
Fill as he also told of successes
Worthy of the world's shallow envy but

The hunched over posture of his body
His absence from a later gathering
And the pain obvious in his words point
To the continuing oppression of

Suffering as it's most difficult to
Overcome neglect during a childhood.

But that's why we come —
to achieve transcendence of
the suffering and
together to turn it to
penetrating compassion.

It's a new world if you're attempting to
Stay sober that appears the same on the
Surface but you'll notice the emotions
Are more painful as if you're a turtle

Who's lost his shell and your skin is tender
And there are people who are angry and
Hurt because of your actions and there's the
Necessity of admitting your wrongs

And repairing the damage and taking
The time to understand the world through the
Eyes of others and so perhaps you'll find
Yourself in a hall of mirrors seeing

Distorted images of whom you thought
You were and discovering you don't know.

It's exploration
attempting to stay sober
and engaging with
life's difficulties — maybe
you'll discover who you are.

It was surprising to realize how
Habitually resentful I had
Become as I was disconnected from
Everything as my mind transformed into

A funnel focusing repeatedly
On why I should be upset excluding
Every mitigating factor and I
Was impervious oblivious and

Cherished justifications and my thoughts
Circulated malignant obsessions
As fuel for alcoholism as I
Drank to escape poisoned thinking — only

Compassionate sober alcoholics
Could transmit the way of sobriety.

The companionship
and shared experience of
my fellow addicts
helped me to surrender my
useless justifications.

Even within the circles of sober
Alcoholics as I gazed about the
Group during those first tenuous months
And years I would catch myself daydreaming

How much happier I'd be if I were
Clever like her or tall like him but I
Knew they're addicts just like me and I had
Greedy eyes and I was compulsively

Comparing myself with them even as
They came to the circles for survival
And I don't know how it happened because
It's a mysterious process but I

Mixed myself with sober alcoholics
And discovered how lovable I am.

The stories and words
had cumulative effect
as I stopped caring
about what I didn't have
and found a home among friends.

During those first few years it felt as though
I were walking out of my life into
The rooms where there was a circle of the
Most welcoming people and addiction

And alcoholism were left outside
With the associated compulsions
And run-away emotions and the so
Dangerous events that had to be faced

While inside we told each other stories
That only fellow-addicts could savor
Properly and we shared a way of life
That fosters transcending growth involving

The replacement of failing habits with
Intuition and appreciation.

As the years have passed
I've come to think differently
And feel differently
And my outlook is open
And my days are engaging.

More than most drunks he has reason for self-
Pity as a young son died suddenly
As grief and anger are persuasive and
So much has disintegrated where's the

Blame in spiraling out of control and
Where's the leverage for trusting a God who
Took a son and yet he's returned to a
Room full of sober alcoholics he's

Listening as we share about hitting
Bottom about how each of us crossed a
Threshold of suffering and surrendered
How together we seek sustenance from

Power beyond ourselves — guidance from a
Wisdom salvaged in the midst of despair.

There's no comparing
of personal suffering —
was it sufficient
for me to surrender and
did it force me to seek help?

He said he went to the casino on
Sunday evenings because the rookies had
Been playing the slots all afternoon so
He went to clean up and in the midst of

His compulsivity while drinking he
Remembered becoming disgusted with
A machine and leaving for another
And colliding with another gambler

On the way and what bothered him today
Was that he said nothing and walked on as
If the other person was nobody
And so many years later within a

Circle of sober alcoholics he
Regretted a moment of rudeness.

Even in the midst
of compulsivity and
a haze of drinking
an addict recognizes
there's a better way to live.

Her husband took many photos she said
And for ten years since his death she's felt a
Reluctance in looking at them because
She wasn't proud of the things that happened —

There was the photo celebrating her
Last day of work at the hospital and
Though she was laughing and cavorting she
Knew how out-of-control drunk she was then —

Here was the denial the stubbornness
The misery she perpetuated —
But there were also the photos of her
Grandchildren who never knew her drinking

During ten years of sobriety — she
Discovered evidence of redemption.

She knew the inside
story of every photo
the pretense and the
reality but she
forgot being redeemed.

I'm a lucky alcoholic who's found
A home within my head and heart and I
Don't have to drink to escape myself and
Don't have to hide from my emotions and

I've learned the tricks necessary to take
Disturbing circumstances and adapt
And I'd rather have a conversation than
A confrontation and I'm more likely

To be spontaneously happy than
Sullen for no explainable reason
Because I've been practicing spiritual
Jujitsu by paying attention to

The quality of my thoughts and often
It's easy to adjust my attitude.

In conversations
with sober alcoholics
I discover ways
of minimizing ego
and letting go of trouble.

I come to mix within the circle of
Sober alcoholics every morning
And the meeting is where my friends are — it's
Where we laugh — and sometimes someone will

Say they have a relative who doesn't
Understand why we come to meetings when
We haven't been drinking for years and it's
Not easy for normal people to see

If I lose my gratitude I'd also
Lose my sobriety and — it's a fact —
Someone in the room is certain to be
Desperate not to drink today and it's good

To bear witness to the suffering and
To communicate how to get sober.

I'm idiosyncratic
and have outlandish stories
that only sober
alcoholics could enjoy
because we've gotten sober.

There are consequences for giving up
If you are alcoholic and you leave
The circle of sober alcoholics
Who have learned to rely on the meetings

Because within any group some of us
Are suffering and others are serene
And as we share experience strength and
Hope the needed words are said and we leave

Encouraged — and as I was exiting
The highway in St. Paul I saw a man
Panhandling on the street and he saw
Me and turned as the recognition was

Painful for both of us — but it's a fact
Those who quit coming become examples.

A bad attitude
stubbornly defiantly
indulged is enough
to send an alcoholic
on the road to his demise.

In circles of sober alcoholics
We laugh spontaneously as we swap
Stories as we enjoy ourselves and make
Light work of sobriety because we

Aren't isolated aren't suffering from
The poisoned thinking characteristic
Of drunk fools so when she confided how
Her father took her to a hospital

How she heard him talking to a nurse in
Another room saying "I don't want her
Anymore" how he tried to leave without
Her but failed we sober alcoholics

Became quiet because we could see the
Budding alcoholism in the girl.

There are stories we
would rather not remember
but we can't forget
so we muster up courage
and tell each other the truth.

Her parents left her behind at a gas
Station and at a swimming pool and they
Didn't intend to hurt her but worse they
Forgot she was one of the family —

And though they retrieved her they also gave
Her the impression she's worthless
And now the grown woman can't get enough
Attention to lose the expectation

She is forgettable — just as if she
Were given a piece of a puzzle and
Assigned the burden of finding where it
Belongs — so it seems she's been abandoned

She's lost and upset and struggling to
Compose herself and to find the way home.

To compose herself
to discover the way home
is quite a puzzle —
in a world full of strangers
to find those who are loving.

We're not all capable of understanding
Each other as I've heard him say that the
Newspaper the television and the
Radio impart private messages

And his skin is continuously stamped
With the imprint of God — and the Devil
Is a presence tormenting his thoughts — and
Jesus is a Savior today and though

We breathe the same air we don't receive the
Same stimulus and he's articulate
Enough to use words rational enough
To describe his thoughts passionate enough

To specify a reality so
Unrecognizable I can't respond.

Perplexity and
passionate intensity
have come together —
he understands just enough
to perceive his separateness.

We finished on Friday afternoon when
Usually our crew would return to
The yard at twilight and I was happy
To be done with asphalt driveways and I

Showered and ate and went to the bar alone
At the beginning of a holiday
Weekend on the Fourth of July — I was
Elated to be young and strong but was

Lonely too amidst strangers feeling out
Of place so I drank like a fool shots
Of tequila and I remember a
Glimpse of lying in a police cruiser —

Of being showered at Ramsey County
Detox — and of waking with a split head.

The drinking was an
attempt at overcoming
disconnection — but
at the time my behavior
was quite unexplainable.

I became an exciting driver near
The end because I never knew where I'd
End up or who I'd meet in the night and
One evening I found myself blundering

In a field though I'd been aiming at the
Road and I sped up — I have a hazy
Recollection of meandering home —
And the last night I sped up a hill in

Stillwater took a sharp turn and faced a
Lighted police cruiser while my friend in
Exasperation was grasping my neck
Politely obliging me to stop so

I went to jail which displeased me so I
Asked to be taken to detox again.

For alcoholics
once drinking's begun there's no
control of how much
of how long or of what could
eventuate on the way.

So much of my experience depends
On my outlook and I found myself at
A detox center again discussing
The situation of my arrival

With earnest volunteers who suggested
Bad things happen when alcoholics drink —
But there is a solution — and I felt
The resistance within vanish — and the

Shame was lifted from my shoulders and for
More than thirty years I've not had a drink
Because in an instant I surrendered
And became willing to do anything

For a better life — and for decades I've
Watched people die before surrendering.

Why was I able
to surrender while many
others couldn't — what's
the mysterious edge
favoring my life?

We discussed how sober alcoholics
Are likely clueless about knowing when
Enough is enough because we often
Want more whether it be excitement or

Praise for our deeds or quantities of goods —
Because why buy one when you can have three? —
And Larry said we are the best worst guys
Or the worst best guys — anyway if we're

Passionate we're compulsive too and don't
Recognize the compulsion and can't be
Otherwise unless somehow we learn to
Jump outside ourselves and see exactly

What we're doing so it helps to bounce our
Separate perspectives off each other.

Because we remain
addicted to excitement
and want to be the
center of attention and
avoid mundaneity.

He told us about being lost in the
Gobi but he wasn't disconcerted
Because he had a guide who knew how to
Bark like a dog and listen — and the guide

Drove over the dunes and stopped and barked and
Listened and drove again — as the stars were
Spectacular — and eventually
They heard the barking in the distance of

A sheep dog leading to the ger of a
Family where he could do what he came
For — to provide medical care — and then
They were directed to Ulaan Baater

Ingenuity will find direction
Wayfarers use sheepdogs in the desert.

A clear head
a willing heart
patience and fortitude
allow unlimited
adventure.

Deer Hunting on Sunday

It's quite cold before dawn — he said — and the
Hollow was much colder and he heard drops
Falling from the trees but couldn't see much
In the gloom — but he remembered how good

The warmth of the sun feels when the body
Is chilled — so with the sun rising with the
Light filtering through the trees he rose and
Walked up hill looking for an opening

And up ahead he saw a log within a
Showering of light and the moisture in
The log was escaping and steaming and
Just for a moment an iridescence

Arose hovering and shimmering and —
The once-in-a-lifetime vision vanished.

He shared his vision
and he shared his gratitude
that he was sober
that he could appreciate
clarity and redemption.

More than a few of us in the circle
Dread the approach of Christmas because the
Season reminds us of regrettable
Memories and sometimes our parents and

Siblings are out-of-control drinkers and
We'd rather not be gathered together —
But he reminisced about the cookies
His mother baked for Christmas of a Czech

Recipe consisting of flour and ground
Walnut — but this year she was ill and in
Bed and he volunteered and he followed
Instructions and when he and a sister

Opened a paper bag of the cookies
They smelled the years of sweetest memories.

Some alcoholics
lug the baggage of Christmas
but sharing stories
is a way to rekindle
buried enthusiasm.

Such things too
the smudges
on slabs

take part in
the bloom —

row apartments
and vine roses.

(Remembering our one-time home in Japan.)

— *Tekkan*

www.ingramcontent.com/pod-product-compliance
Lightning Source LLC
Chambersburg PA
CBHW070519010526
44118CB00012B/1032